Jodi —

SAVING MINDS, SAVING SOULS

Thank you so much for your support and your witness!

[illegible]

SAVING MINDS, SAVING SOULS

REVITALIZING CATHOLIC EDUCATION THROUGH WITNESS

SARAH THOMAS

NEW DEGREE PRESS

SAVING MINDS, SAVING SOULS

Revitalizing Catholic Education Through Witness

ISBN 979-8-88504-970-2 *Paperback*

979-8-88504-971-9 *Kindle Ebook*

979-8-88504-972-6 *Ebook*

To my teachers, classmates, colleagues, and students,
whose witness continues to inspire me.

CONTENTS

But above all with your life be witnesses of what you communicate. Educators [...] pass on knowledge and values with their words; but their words will have an incisive effect on children and young people if they are accompanied by their witness, their consistent way of life.

POPE FRANCIS

ADDRESS TO THE STUDENTS OF THE JESUIT SCHOOLS OF ITALY AND ALBANIA, 2013

INTRODUCTION

In the darkness of the auditorium, the projector screen's bluish-gray light cast ominous shadows on the faces of the teachers peppering the seats. Some stared transfixed at the screen. Others diligently took notes as fast as they could, striving to keep up with the pace of the presentation. Most of the rest surreptitiously (or not-so-surreptitiously) checked emails, graded electronically submitted assignments, or put together practice schedules and team rosters for upcoming athletic events. A colleague to my right attempted a little bit of all three, deftly shifting from team mom emails and the week's varsity workout regimen to lesson plans for an upcoming unit.

I found myself fidgeting as the presentation dragged on. In between glances at my colleague's workout schedule and scanning the room for the tell-tale nodding heads of professional development dozers, my teeth started to clench. The expert consultant hired to speak to us for our in-service day extolled the benefits of "the prevalence of data and the quantified self," intoning with the enthusiasm only a consultant could muster, "What we measure... improves." While

I did not necessarily disagree with the sentiment, I began to brood over the profound incompatibility between our school's efforts to educate the "whole child" while simultaneously reducing our students to data points. I cringed as the buzzwords echoed through the auditorium: Data. Measurability. Assessment. Value proposition. Enrollment retention. Eventually, I couldn't take it anymore. I pulled out my school-issued Chromebook, opened an incognito window so I could gain access to my personal email account and Google Drive, and began typing furiously.

What we need is better catechesis, I wrote. *And that includes us. That is what we should be doing.*

I would later find out that the hired consultant was affiliated with a Catholic organization and had more than three decades' worth of experience in Catholic schools. The presentation itself, however, remained firmly grounded in educational trends and theories I had already learned about in the teacher education course required both for state certification and my continued employment at the school. Nothing I heard or saw during the presentation seemed explicitly Catholic.

In fact, by October 2019, I had been teaching in a Catholic school for fourteen months and had yet to participate in professional development focused on how to teach in a Catholic school. The previous fall, all the Catholic educators in the state had convened at my school for a two-day conference; however, because my school had used state funding to pay the faculty's registration fees, most of us were told not to register for any of the specifically Catholic sessions. (The theology teachers were exempt since the Catholic-focused sessions were integral to their area of study.) With the chaos of session transitions and the lack of attendance-taking and sign-ins at the beginning of most sessions, I know of several colleagues who attended the Catholic-focused sessions anyway. Aside from the annual faculty retreat that focused on our spiritual needs and growth, though, our professional development consisted almost entirely of education theory and application rather than on integrating said education theory and application into our work as Catholic educators.

I struggled with festering disenchantment despite my efforts to remain positive. After dreaming of teaching in a Catholic school for close to a decade, the reality of my day-to-day routine often left me feeling like a stranger in a strange land. My thirteen years spent as a student in Catholic schools seemed, in some respects, utterly foreign to my current surroundings, and the resulting whiplash left me disoriented. More than anything, I was becoming increasingly uncomfortable with the small voice in the back of my head whispering insistently, "Are we, in fact, little more than a public school that prays a lot?" *Something has to change*, I thought. *But what? Where on earth should it begin?*

Over the last half-century, the Catholic education landscape has changed significantly. According to the National Catholic Educational Association's *Annual Statistical Report on Schools, Enrollment and Staffing*, 11,000 Catholic schools educated 5.5 million students in the United States in 1960. Today, 5,500 Catholic schools educate 1.6 million students. Ian Lovett, in his May 2020 article for the *Wall Street Journal*, reports that sources confirmed "at least 209 Catholic schools across the country have closed in the past year [2020]." Lovett also reports that enrollment in Catholic schools saw a 6.4 percent decline at the start of the 2020–2021 school year, the largest decline since the 1970s. Individual Catholic dioceses have seen different trends in their own numbers—the *Word on Fire Show*'s episode "The Future of Catholic Schools" notes that urban Catholic schools and those in the Northeast and Midwest have been hit particularly hard, whereas Catholic schools elsewhere in the country have seen stable and/or increasing enrollment over the last eighteen months. The overarching narrative, however, is one of serving fewer students in fewer schools. The explanations for this decline stretch beyond the realm of education and appear in greater detail later in this book, but for the moment, a couple of touchstones are worth mentioning.

Many of the challenges facing Catholic education stem from a single question: "Why should I spend the money on a Catholic education for my child(ren)?" The question itself seems reasonable enough, as do the potential motivations behind it. The first of these motivations is a practical one. According to the National Alliance for Public Charter Schools, more than 7,700 public charter schools currently exist in the United States and serve more than 3.4 million students. The National Home Education Research Institute, meanwhile, reports that the number of households choosing home education for their children has been increasing since the 1970s. Setting aside the sharp increase in homeschooling households since March 2020, the homeschooled student population nevertheless has seen steady increases of 2 to 8 percent over the last several years. Given the growth of public school alternatives such as these, even the affordability of Catholic schools compared to other private schools appears expensive.

Despite these phenomena, however, the most common answer to the question is that Catholic schools offer a "better education." The metrics for "better" have been both myriad and contested, according to Mai Miksic. Advocacy groups have long touted Catholic school students' stronger performance on standardized testing, higher college acceptance rates, and higher four-year college graduation rates compared with their public school counterparts. At the same time, though, some researchers have questioned the correlation between these results and the Catholic schools themselves. For at least the last twenty-five years, studies have attempted to discern the degree to which phenomena such as selection bias might affect these results. Other scholars and studies have interrogated the long-term benefits of Catholic education on metrics such as reading and writing scores, with some demonstrating diminishing gains over time. Within such a statistical milieu and given the pressures from educational alternatives, Catholic schools find themselves in a delicate position: they have to present themselves as competitive and relevant, and they have to continue to demonstrate how what they offer is "worth the money."

I agree that Catholic schools offer a "better education" than many of the available alternatives. That "better education," however, doesn't necessarily translate to the data points so beloved by educational researchers and professional development gurus. Rather, as Kathleen Porter-Magee and Raymond Domanico of the Manhattan Institute noted in 2019, "being 'Catholic on the inside' is more important to the long-term outcomes that we want for students." For Porter-Magee and Domanico, "Catholic on the inside" refers to the values system that undergirds Catholic schools: the "way they treat every student as having equal worth before God." Putting this emphasis solidly and unabashedly at the forefront of Catholic schools is vital to their continued survival. It's something we cannot lose sight of, even as we continue to position ourselves as a competitive, relevant investment in young people's development and success. It should be readily discernible, an ethos permeating the Catholic school beyond the sacramentals on the walls or the crests emblazoned on the uniforms. It should radiate from each faculty and staff member at the school. And witness is the key.

After my "Aha!" moment in October 2019, I couldn't shake the growing conviction that I needed to say something, explore the reasons behind the impressions I had of twenty-first century Catholic schools, and investigate possible pathways for the better catechesis I believed my colleagues and I needed in order to fulfill our responsibilities—what we might call our "vocations"—as Catholic educators. Driven by my personal interest and frustration, I began to write about the things I observed in school and my teacher certification program. I perused websites, stumbled across blogs, and commiserated with colleagues. Even in the company of my supervisors, I tried to frame my feedback in constructive ways, despite the vitriolic thoughts running through my head.

Along the way, what had begun as (self-)righteous indignation at the seeming travesty I was witnessing shifted to compassion. I realized that in order to keep our doors open and remain responsible stewards of our resources, some of the decisions against which I initially railed actually attempted to balance the school's faith-based mission with the realities of operating a school in the twenty-first century. However, while compromises may be necessary at times, we must acknowledge when and where they could also compromise the integrity of what Catholic schools stand for. Understanding the various ways this balancing act plays out is at the heart of this book.

I hope this book will familiarize readers with some of the key issues facing Catholic schools today and will explain why the integrated, interpersonal approach I am calling "witness" lies at the heart of the potential solutions to these issues. By drawing on my own experiences in Catholic schools, interviews with educators and administrators, and research into the state of education more broadly and Catholic education more specifically, I will outline how our current cultural moment has positioned Catholic education for a renaissance. Those already within the Catholic school community will find this book of particular interest, but it is not exclusively for an already-Catholic audience. Families considering Catholic schools for their children will find this book useful as they explore educational options, and people interested in understanding "what makes Catholic schools different" will gain insight from the engaging narratives in these pages.

Saving Minds, Saving Souls is about what we can do to revitalize Catholic education by embracing the intersections of culture, education, and faith.

CHAPTER 1

"FOLLOW THE MONEY"

"When in doubt, follow the money."

Our students bent their heads over their notebooks and dutifully copied down the phrase, then looked expectantly up at Leah, my co-teacher. We were teaching an interdisciplinary honors-level humanities class to tenth-grade students at my first high-school teaching job, several years before I joined a Catholic school faculty. Leah served as the AP Art History teacher and director of arts for our school, and she had primary responsibility for the course's artistic content. With my English literature background, I took the lead when delivering the literature content. Over the course of the year, we explored possible answers to a single essential question—"What does it mean to be human?"—by examining written, visual, and architectural "texts" produced by richly varied cultures at different moments throughout history. Using this concept of "text as cultural artifact," we encouraged our students to understand how texts can reveal the values of the people who create and use them. We had a blast, and I miss teaching it.

As we worked our way from the magnificence of Hammurabi's *stele* to the flying buttresses of European cathedrals, Leah continued to remind students to "follow the money." She usually made the comment within the context of encouraging our students to understand the role of patronage in the history of art: Who makes it? What purpose does it serve? For whom is it made? In our non-sectarian/secular school, many of our students would ask about the prevalence of religious images we studied, particularly during our units on the medieval and Renaissance periods. The paintings and sculptures commissioned by families like the Medici and the Pazzi or Michelangelo's commission for the Sistine Chapel ceiling all point to the financial and cultural power of Florentine merchant families and the Roman Catholic Church during the fourteenth and fifteenth centuries. If the Renaissance patronage system provided artists and authors with the means to make a living and opportunities to share their crafts, however, it also allowed the patrons themselves the opportunity to burnish their reputations and gain additional influence through their public visibility as supporters of the arts. It is not only the text that matters; the *con*text matters too. At least, that was what we hoped our students would come to understand.

The circumstances might be different, but Leah's advice to "follow the money" becomes an important consideration when trying to understand some of the challenges facing Catholic education today. At the risk of stretching the metaphor, the questions of "patronage" can apply to the American education system broadly and the Catholic school system in particular: Who makes it? What purpose does it serve? And for whom is it made?

"FOLLOW THE MONEY": BUILDING A CATHOLIC SCHOOL (WHO MAKES IT?)

Since the first "common schools" appeared in Massachusetts in the early nineteenth century, the answers to the "follow the money" questions have largely remained the same. The public school system has, for the most part, been authorized and funded by local, state, and federal legislation. According to the Center on Education Policy at the George Washington University, most funding for public schools comes from state and local revenues, while the remainder—approximately 8 percent—comes from the federal level. The goals of the American education system have also remained largely consistent over the past two centuries: to prepare students for citizenship and work, thereby contributing to the continued prospering of the American ethos and economy.

For Catholic schools in America, the answers to these questions are a little bit different. The Catholic Church has a long, rich scholastic history, from the medieval *scriptoria* where monks crafted illuminated manuscripts to the establishment and staffing of universities still in existence today (of which Georgetown University is the oldest continually operating such institution in the United States). Many of the Catholic elementary and secondary schools in the United States today, though, owe their existence to the rapid expansion of Catholic schools during the first part of the twentieth century. In part a reaction to the explicitly Protestant nature of the moral/civil component of public education and overt anti-Catholic bias in public school settings, the expansion of the Catholic elementary and secondary school network allowed families the opportunity to have their children educated in an environment compatible with their faith. As such, the Catholic schools developed during this time received funding through parish subsidies supported by the Catholic church with the intention of educating children in a manner consistent with Church teaching.

One of the benefits of the development toward promoting equity for all through education came in the form of federal legislation passed during the second half of the twentieth century. The Elementary and Secondary Education Act (ESEA), initially passed in 1965 as part of President Johnson's War on Poverty, states among its goals "strengthen[ing] and improv[ing] educational quality and educational opportunities in the [nation's] elementary and secondary schools." This legislation's successors, the No Child Left Behind Act (NCLB) passed in 2001 and the Every Student Succeeds Act (ESSA) passed in 2015, have reauthorized ESEA while adding provisions and accountability measures to ensure that students of all backgrounds and educational needs have access to high-quality education from qualified teachers. All versions of this legislation provide for the educational needs of children enrolled in private schools, often through coordinating efforts between a local educational agency and a representative for the private school(s) in the same area. Seemingly, this recognition of equitable access to educational resources is a good thing; students should not be discriminated against based on where they happen to attend school.

In our current moment when operating costs for Catholic schools continue to rise even as enrollment numbers nation-wide decline, the availability of these funds might initially seem like a godsend. However, when the government provides funds for such opportunities, strings are attached. All versions of this legislation, from the ESEA to the ESSA, have included the stipulation that "such educational services or other benefits, including materials and equipment, shall be *secular, neutral, and nonideological*" (emphasis added). In other words, faith-based private schools cannot use government funding for purposes that others could perceive as advancing the faith-based mission of the school. The intention behind this stipulation appears reasonable in its own right, particularly in light of the separation of church and state that has become one of the touchstones of the American experience. The end result, however, presents a conundrum for Catholic education: schools with ample "secular," "neutral," and "nonideological" training and resources and comparatively meager material on how to be *Catholic* schools.

"FOLLOW THE MONEY": STAFFING A CATHOLIC SCHOOL (WHAT PURPOSE DOES IT SERVE?)

Many Catholic schools identify both the academic and religious impetuses of their institutions in their mission statements and branding materials: they not only provide rigorous, often college-preparatory curricula in order to prepare students for life beyond the classroom, they also "transform lives in Christ," "form disciples," or otherwise indicate they educate children within a Catholic anthropology and with an eye toward those students having a positive impact on the world as adults. In order to do so, the faculty teaching in Catholic schools need to be prepared to undertake both the academic and spiritual formation of their students.

With this undertaking in mind, shifts in the Catholic school professoriate that coincide with the other trends already addressed in this chapter must receive attention as well. The National Catholic Educational Association's annual reports include historical data on US Catholic school faculty demographics. In 1960, 73.8 percent of Catholic school teachers in the United States were "religious/clergy" (priests, nuns, brothers, members of religious orders, etc.); only 26.2 percent of Catholic school teachers at the time were lay people (not religious/clergy). By 2021, a mere 2.3 percent of Catholic school teachers in the United States were religious/clergy, while 97.7 percent were lay people. These numbers follow an overall decline in the number of religious vocations (people choosing to become religious/clergy) over the past several decades; so in that sense, they are not out of the ordinary. They do, however, have significant ramifications for Catholic education.

For religious/clergy who teach in Catholic schools, such endeavors often count as part of their vocation or ministry—in other words, their "work" for the Catholic Church. In addition, Catholic priests, nuns, and brothers do not marry; furthermore, they often live in communities and thus have most of their housing and living needs met. As a result, salary and compensation packages look different than they do for lay teachers who have to support themselves and their families. Put another way, one of the factors contributing to rising operating costs for Catholic schools lies in the need to offer precisely these kinds of competitive salary and compensation packages to their lay employees.

In addition to accounting for the effect of a predominately lay professoriate on operating costs, "following the money" needs to consider the financial effects of professional training for Catholic school faculty. Ensuring the success of both academic and religious endeavors often places the emphasis on the former rather than the latter. In an effort to ensure Catholic school faculty are "highly qualified" (a designation often made and enforced by state credentialing agencies), it is not unusual for Catholic schools to require their faculty to hold state certification—either as a prerequisite for hiring or as a requirement to be completed within a specified time frame after joining the faculty. When it comes to assisting teachers with procuring the requisite state certification after joining a Catholic school, locating and paying for the necessary programs or coursework leads back to ESSA. Title II of this legislation aims to increase student achievement through several initiatives, including through improving faculty quality and effectiveness.

Ensuring all students have the opportunity to benefit from the provisions of this legislation is a worthy endeavor, as is developing teachers and administrators who can effectively meet the educational needs of the students and encourage improvement in student achievement. It therefore makes sense that Catholic schools would avail themselves of the funding provided through federal legislation such as ESSA. Given the limitations of said funding's uses, however, many Catholic school teachers are trained in secular programs that do not account for the distinct needs of Catholic school faculties. These specific needs subsequently must be addressed through other avenues.

"FOLLOW THE MONEY": FILLING A CATHOLIC SCHOOL (FOR WHOM IS IT MADE?)

The ripple effects of "following the money" from making and staffing Catholic schools overflow into the matter of filling Catholic schools. Many Catholic schools in the United States operate on a tuition model. According to the National Catholic Educational Association, average tuition costs per student during the 2019–2020 school year covered approximately 82.3 percent of the actual education costs for elementary schools and approximately 64.7 percent for high schools. Tuition assistance is available at the vast majority of these schools. Subsidies, development efforts, and fundraising make up the difference.

Because families pay a portion of the actual cost to educate their children in Catholic schools, "following the money" in order to fill a Catholic school requires an understanding of the demographic landscape in which Catholic schools operate. It should come as no great shock to many that the number of adults in the United States who eschew a specific religious affiliation has increased markedly in recent years. Where Catholics were once the single largest religious denomination in the country, they now account for little more than 20 percent of the population. Meanwhile, the so-called "Nones" according to the Pew Research Center and others—those who self-identify as having no religious affiliation—are currently the fastest growing (non)religious demographic in the country. The most recent data available suggests approximately a quarter of the US population falls into this group.

Amid such a cultural shift away from religious affiliation, who chooses Catholic education for their children? Who becomes the prospective student population for Catholic schools? And why would Catholic schools be a particularly attractive choice? Certainly, all families who desire to educate their children in Catholic schools should be able to do so. Furthermore, Catholic schools have always been open to educating students who are not Catholic, and such openness can and should continue. Catholic schools today, however, must also contend with the effects that the rising number of "Nones" could have on their student populations. Before these effects can be considered, though, students have to enroll first.

When considering the growth and educational needs of the "Nones," "following the money" necessitates an understanding of how and why parents choose a particular school for their children. Quentin Wodon, for example, has published an analysis of parental priorities regarding their children's education for the *Journal of Catholic Education*. Using a 2018 market research report as his starting point, Wodon highlights, "To survive [...] Catholic schools will need to demonstrate that they provide students with a distinctive educational experience that responds to parental priorities for what children should learn in schools." This demonstration should appeal both to parents whose children already attend Catholic schools and to those open to Catholic schools but whose children do not (yet) attend them. Among what he calls "heterogeneous" parental priorities, critical thinking, preparation for college and the job market, communications skills, and embracing diversity are the most important for the

"Nones." While Wodon recommends continuing to emphasize and strengthen academic excellence and deepening students' faith, he also notes that "if the deepening of the faith in Catholic schools is done in a manner that does not respect diversity—including diversity in religious beliefs—this may exacerbate a perception that Catholic schools not only may lack diversity in their student body, but that they may also not be welcoming for all."

Another way to think of the priorities noted by Wodon and others is cultural relevance. In these instances, "following the money" includes responding to parental priorities in light of shifting demographics and their effects on Catholic school enrollment. Clearly communicating how schools balance cultural relevance and parental priorities with adherence to Church teachings is key to sustaining and revitalizing Catholic education.

WITNESS AND "FOLLOWING THE MONEY"

For Leah and me, "following the money" in the humanities classroom provided a mechanism for our students to understand the exigence of a text—how the creator, audience, and purpose all interact at the moment of a text's creation. From that starting point, we then encouraged our students to consider how the text's original purpose aligns with how a twenty-first century audience understands the same text. In much the same way, "following the money" hopefully has offered a similar framework for comprehending the current landscape of Catholic education. Granted, papal patronage of Renaissance artists and archdiocesan subsidies/parent tuition payments for Catholic schools might not quite be horses of the same color. The Medici influence on Florentine politics might not be a perfect parallel for the "Nones" of the twenty-first century, either. In both cases, however, the interplay of such dynamic forces must be acknowledged.

Bearing witness to these factors by acknowledging them is the first step toward embracing teaching at the intersections of culture, education, and faith.

CHAPTER 2

THE MISSION MATRIX

"So, why do you want to work in an independent school?" Jacob asked as he settled himself at the opposite end of the bench.

Midway through my on-campus interview for my first high school teaching job, I welcomed the opportunity for a comparatively informal one-on-one conversation after a morning of group meetings with students and potential colleagues. A longtime English teacher had decided over the summer not to return for the coming school year, leaving the school scrambling to advertise, interview, and hire a new teacher in only six weeks. I had completed the first two rounds of the interview process over the phone. Alternating between sitting cross-legged on my couch and pacing the beige shag carpet in my graduate school apartment, I played up my teaching credentials and squeezed as much advantage as I could out of the sixth-degree connections my interviewers and I had discovered during our conversations. Now, I sat on a wooden bench in an idyllic Tudor revival courtyard, trying to assure myself I was glowing rather than sweating in the late July heat.

I immediately liked Jacob upon meeting him in person. His openness and unpretentious approach to his responsibilities as the upper school head belied his intelligence and the probity of his questions. *I think we could work well together*, I thought to myself as he showed me around the campus before taking me to the courtyard. Sitting outside for his portion of the on-campus interview had been his idea.

"Well, one of the things I've always valued in independent school education is its mission-driven focus. I want to work for an organization that has a clear sense of its purpose and calibrates itself accordingly," I said.

"And your own experience in independent schools has been in religiously affiliated ones, correct?"

"Yes, it has. Thirteen years of Catholic school. I've often joked that plaid is my favorite color." I grinned as charmingly as I could as I said it.

He chuckled and crossed one ankle across his knee as he draped an arm over the back of the bench. "How do you feel about the prospect of working in a non-sectarian school, then? What do you foresee as a possible challenge facing a non-sectarian or secular independent school?"

I squinted as I gazed into the middle distance. "I think," I began, weighing my next words carefully, "the challenge of a non-sectarian or secular independent school lies in agreeing on the ethos at the heart of the mission statement." I took his thoughtful nod as encouragement and continued. "That's where parochial schools might have an advantage: the ethos, or the central or founding principles of the school's mission, have a clear source that is greater than any one member of the community. I think that kind of clarity can provide stability that works to the community's advantage."

"I see," he said, still nodding. I hesitated before deciding to keep going.

"That's not to say non-sectarian or secular independent schools can't accomplish something similar, but I do think they need to be very thoughtful and deliberate about how they determine what that ethos is so that it doesn't become subject to the whims of any given moment." I paused again. "I'm eager to be part of those conversations."

The furrow in his forehead relaxed, and he grinned broadly. "That's great," he said. "I'm glad to hear that." I smiled back.

INTO THE MATRIX: THE MISSION (STATEMENT) CONUNDRUM

On reflection, Jacob's questions about how I understood the differences between independent and Catholic schools were prescient. The relaxed forehead and the grin I had noticed at the end of our conversation turned out to be harbingers of an eventual request to serve on an academic affairs committee tasked with articulating what a graduate of our pre-K–12 school should look like. In those committee meetings and in one-on-one conferences, Jacob and I continued returning to the relationship between the school's mission statement and the day-to-day decision-making essential to keeping a school running. We were not alone in our efforts. In fact, much ink and time have been spent discussing the importance of school mission statements, particularly for independent and Catholic schools. The attention given to these documents and their particularities seems to reach a curious consensus:

1. Mission statements are invaluable tools, particularly for private/independent schools, to articulate their purpose and goals to themselves and their communities.
2. Mission statements are notorious for being poorly written—so poorly, in fact, as to be essentially useless.

These two phenomena, particularly the latter, have multiple explanations. Experts such as Peter Gow, who has spent more than forty years as a teacher and administrator in independent schools, have stressed the importance of "the need for some kind of pole star or driving impetus [...] if the [independent] school is to have any coherence in its purposes, its programs, and its culture." For Gow, the mission statement provides the "pole star" that can guide and ground the independent school. Given its vital importance, however, he also admits mission statements have become "highly susceptible to both parody and banality." On this point, Gow agrees with other educational mission statement experts, including Skip Kotkins of independent school recruiting firm Carney Sandoe & Associates and Greg Bamford of the National Association of Independent Schools. Kotkins goes so far as to suggest that bad mission statements are endemic to the independent school. Bamford adds to the critique by suggesting "mission statements often become long lists of everything a school aspires to be," rather than what they currently are. In either case, they become difficult to fully realize. Both experts acknowledge that the practical realities and anxieties of "following the money"—distinguishing one school from another in a competitive educational marketplace—often impede rather than invigorate the mission statement crafting process.

In general, I agree with the laments of those who highlight the shortcomings of the mission statement. Inclined to fall prey either to the hopelessly, unproductively generic and the platitudinous or to the circuitous, vapid diction and syntax choices that obfuscate rather than clarify, mission statements often sound better than they work. Perhaps these flaws are, to some extent, reflective of the degree to which the mission statement is "performative": rather than (or in addition to) trying to "brand" a school for marketing and enrollment purposes, the mission statement instead signals that a school can "keep up with the times." The potential disadvantage to this focus, rather than on clearly articulating the school's purpose and goals, is that the resulting effort lacks conviction and follow-through. Lest a school seem out of step and therefore a poor choice for prospective families, the mission statement becomes a "thing to have" rather than a "thing to be." It becomes, in essence, an exercise in vanity rather than in purpose. Moreover, they become subject to the whims of any given moment. As the lingo changes, as the educational fads change, as the presumptions of prospective families change, so too must the "now-focused" mission statement. The mission statement should be both more fully grounded and more aspirational than the elusive popularity of a single moment or application and enrollment season.

For these independent school experts and others, a perceived solution lies in distinguishing "mission" from "mission statement." Bamford, for example, notes "a crisp, distinctive mission that evokes the core of a school makes it easier for every board member to remember: *What does our mission call us to do?* [...] The school clarifies its powerful, pithy reason to exist. And boards begin having better conversations." If mission is the raison d'être and the mission statement articulates that raison d'être, then understanding a school's mission, of course, should precede trying to articulate that mission in a statement. Even here, though, the terms appear to be used interchangeably, so it's not clear if the board of trustees decides the school's raison d'être or merely serves as its custodians. If the former, then like so many other things, the mission risks becoming subject to the whims of the board members at any given time. If the latter, then the necessity of distinguishing between "mission" and "mission statement" becomes unclear, unless it's because the language used to articulate that mission must be clear rather than obfuscatory and should, at its core, be able to withstand the pendulum swings of educational fad-losophies.

FAD-LOSOPHY OR FALLACY?

A few years after that fateful July conversation with Jacob, I sat opposite the Head of School, Seth, in a coffee shop for my annual one-on-one faculty chat. I recognized the value in engaging with the faculty in this more relaxed way, though I had begun to approach the meetings with more apprehension than enthusiasm. The previous year, Seth had told me that my suggestions regarding student discipline were incongruous with the school mission's commitment to educating students toward moral, academic, artistic, and athletic excellence. Educating students *toward* moral excellence, I had been admonished, meant not *expecting* moral excellence from the outset. The comments still stung a year later.

"So, what are you proud of this year?" Seth asked as I settled into the bistro chair opposite him with my steaming caffè mocha.

"I'm proud of myself for surviving the school year. Taking on two new preps in the same year, including one outside my subject area, was hard. But the students learned what I set out for them to learn, so I consider that a win for the year."

"That's good!" he said, sipping his coffee as he scribbled notes on his legal pad. "Anything else?"

"No, that's it, I think," I said, smiling.

"Well, then, what do you think we're doing well?"

"I think we've done a pretty good job at fostering community. One of the things I've come to love about working in a pre-K–12 school is watching the relationships between the oldest and the youngest students, particularly when we have our all-school service learning days. I know my seniors grumble about having to participate, but watching them interact with their lower-school 'buddies' is really heartwarming," I said.

"Great, that's great. I think that program is really starting to find its feet," Seth said. He paused briefly before asking, "And what do you think needs to change?"

I took a deep breath. *Here we go again*, I thought. "I think we could be doing a better job of clarifying our mission and identity to the broader community."

"What do you mean?"

"I mean that there seems to be some confusion about whether we're a secular school—"

"We're not," he said. "We're non-sectarian."

"Really? Then I think that needs to be made more clear." His eyes narrowed thoughtfully. I took this as permission to continue. "And I think that, until we figure out and clarify that, we'll struggle on a day-to-day basis with making sure what we're doing has clear connections to our mission."

"In what ways?" Seth stopped taking notes and looked up at me.

"Well, in consistently implementing disciplinary procedures, for one. If it starts to look like 'moral excellence' looks different based on the circumstances or the people involved, then trust in the process—the honor code, in particular—will start to erode." His eyebrows lifted. "Ultimately, who determines what 'moral excellence' looks like?" I could feel my ears getting hot, and my hands started to sweat.

"We do. The community."

"But doesn't that turn something like 'moral excellence' into a moving target, if it's subject to the whims of the particular members of the community at any given time? How does a school maintain consistency and focus in those circumstances?" *I didn't mean to turn this meeting into a philosophical debate. All I want to do is have my thirty-minute meeting and go home*, I thought.

"Look, I don't think that being able to justify a decision by saying 'the Church says so' is helpful. Sitting in a meeting with a student and his parents and pointing to James 5:13 isn't going to make things any easier. In fact, to believe that it does is a fallacy." He half-smiled as he leaned back in his chair.

My heart started pounding. *Did he seriously just call my entire K–12 educational experience a fallacy?* I considered storming out of the coffee shop but instead kept my seat and held his gaze, my own eyes hardening. His face reddened slightly. "I didn't mean to imply that parochial schools are bad for believing so," he said. "Truly, I didn't mean to offend you." I remained silent, hoping he couldn't see my hand tremble as I took a sip of lukewarm mocha.

THE MISSION OF CATHOLIC SCHOOLS: WHAT MAKES THEM DIFFERENT

I never did ask Seth what he meant by referring to the basis of parochial school discipline as a fallacy. As often happens when I find myself in an impromptu debate, I struggled to articulate my objections to Seth's claim. In the moment, I understood "fallacy" as Merriam-Webster's sense of "a false or mistaken idea." It seemed to critique more than my own educational background; it cut to the heart of my entire worldview. The feeling of invalidation that swept through me was troubling for at least two reasons. First, I assumed the comment meant that understanding how to approach the world through the lessons learned from scripture was an erroneous one. Following from the first assumption, I then inferred that either deriving a school's mission from scripture or pointing a school's mission back toward scripture was a mistake. How could grounding a school's mission—and, by extension, the day-to-day decisions guided by that mission—in something bigger than the school itself be a mistake?

In one sense, Seth was correct. Parochial schools are not automatically exempt from all the challenges faced by other schools. Among such challenges are those that come with striving for relevance in an increasingly competitive school landscape, including the crafting of mission statements that clearly and accurately convey the school's ethos. While not immune to the potential pitfalls mentioned earlier, though, Catholic schools start the mission statement crafting process from a much stronger position; they already have a built-in mission. As part of the Catholic Church, they have the highest purpose. The Vatican's Sacred Congregation for Catholic Education, in its 1977 publication *The Catholic School*, identifies the definition and purpose of the Catholic school as follows:

> *The Catholic school forms part of the saving mission of the Church, especially for education in the faith. Remembering that "the simultaneous development of man's psychological and moral consciousness is demanded by Christ almost as a pre-condition for the reception of the befitting divine gifts of truth and grace," the Church fulfills her obligation to foster in*

her children a full awareness of their rebirth to a new life. It is precisely in the Gospel of Christ, taking root in the minds and lives of the faithful, that the Catholic school finds its definition as it comes to terms with the cultural conditions of the times.

The Catholic school, then, has a two-fold mission. It is at once *evangelical* (responsible for teaching young people in the Catholic faith, specifically the "good news" as contained in scripture) and *academic* (responsible for cultivating knowledge and critical thinking skills that help young people understand the world around them). The Sacred Congregation for Catholic Education reiterates this dual purpose in *The Catholic School on the Threshold of the Third Millennium*, written on the twentieth anniversary of *The Catholic School*:

The complexity of the modern world makes it all the more necessary to increase awareness of the ecclesial identity of the Catholic school. [...] The Catholic school participates in the evangelizing mission of the Church and is the privileged environment in which Christian education is carried out. In this way, "Catholic schools are at once places of evangelization, of complete formation, of inculturation, of apprenticeship in a lively dialogue between young people of different religions and social backgrounds." The ecclesial nature of the Catholic school, therefore, is written in the very heart of its identity as a teaching institution. It remains a true and proper ecclesial entity by reason of its educational activity, "in which faith, culture, and life are brought into harmony."

How, then, should Catholic schools approach articulating their mission? Even if one chooses to follow the suggestions of experts like Kotkins and Gow, Catholic schools already have the tools necessary for success at their disposal. For example, the "pole star" identified by Gow that should serve as the basis for articulating mission can be found in the rich tradition of the Church's history and teaching authority (also known as the *magisterium*). While some people might raise concerns that this richness of tradition creates an essential sameness among all Catholic schools and therefore among Catholic school mission statements, it is more productive to see this similarity as a strength rather than a weakness.

Furthermore, if one were to try to build additional documentation to articulate the exigence of the Catholic school using Kotkins's "Portrait of a Graduate," the answer here also seems all too clear. As "the *output* that the school hopes to achieve," the Portrait of a Graduate makes clear why the school exists: to "graduate students who look like this portrait." In the case of Catholic schools, the Portrait of a Graduate should be clear. Catholic schools want to create *saints*. By "saint," I am referring to the meaning of "holy" or "set apart"—for heaven, yes, but also for engaging with the world in such a way that "faith, culture, and life are brought into harmony" because, as Mark Hart has said in his article "Saints in the Making," they have not held anything back.

It would seem Catholic schools have a clear advantage over other kinds of schools. Even so, the connection between aspiration and reality, between the ideal and the real, still requires delicate navigation. In essence, it requires witness.

WITNESS AND MISSION

"Discovering the school's mission" and "creating the school's mission" are slippery terms. Moreover, the phrases seem to be at odds with each other. The process of "discovering the school's mission" suggests the greater purpose (or the aspirational aim, to use Bamford's language) already exists for a school; it suggests something of the custodial nature of a board of trustees. In Catholic terms, it suggests the stewardship that ought to lie at the organization's heart. By contrast, "creating a school's mission"—particularly for an extant school—seems potentially backward. It bends the institution to the trustees' will, rather than placing the institution itself (not to mention the institution's purpose) at the center.

Whether "discovering" or "creating," however, part of Bamford's work in advocating for stronger independent school mission statements lies in encouraging schools to realize that crafting the mission (statement) is only the first part of the process. While it's helpful to "create shared language [so] it's easier for your community to hold on to the things that matter," he correctly notes the essential work actually lies in putting the mission (statement) into action. Putting a school's mission into action in concrete and readily recognizable ways is vital work, and it should always remain at the forefront of a school's day-to-day actions. Indeed, to do so is to bear witness to the mission of the school.

Although I bristled in the moment, I came to realize Seth's comment about running a school not being easier because of the ability to cite scripture has some truth to it. The complexities of running a school transcend creed and governing board makeup, and the ability to blithely advise a student body to pray when "anyone among you is suffering" (as James 5:13 instructs) is not by itself a panacea for all issues that may arise. However, Catholic schools *do* benefit from the "shared language" of the church, indeed making "hold[ing] on to the things that matter" a much clearer undertaking. The real work of bearing witness to the mission of the Catholic school lies in embracing and teaching at the intersections of culture, education, and faith.

CHAPTER 3

THE VALUE OF EXPERIENCE

The Galleria exhibit hall teemed with life. Its stuffiness felt at odds with the sheer size of the space. It also was a sharp contrast to the February chill that had cut through my jacket and blouse on the walk up from the parking garage. Anxious job candidates milled about the hallways, nervously adjusting their ill-fitting suits: the shirt collars that wouldn't lie quite flat; the tie knot that kept shifting just off-center; the skirts that kept twisting whenever the candidates took more than three steps. *Does the last button of a three-button suit jacket need to be buttoned or not? Not, I think, but I haven't worn a suit since my great-aunt's funeral.* Regardless of pedigree, the shifting in rarely worn, barely broken-in dress shoes united all in the choreography of anticipation, an ensemble arranging itself in starting positions for a career-making performance.

Once the doors opened, everyone rushed forward. Heads bobbed as candidates from all walks of life attempted to translate the provided tidy diagram and participating schools roster to the maelstrom they now faced. My friend and I, falsely secure in our familiarity with the organization hosting the job fair, hugged each other around our shoulder bags and portfolios, carefully avoiding the freshly printed résumés and cover letters we had prepared that morning. "Good luck," I said to her.

"You too. See you outside in an hour," she said. "If I finish before you, I'll try to find you. Be thinking about where you want to eat."

"Will do!" I called back to her and dove into the crowd.

The school I sought occupied a table at the back of the hall, but I tried not to let the distance unnerve me as I navigated the maze of tables, personnel, and candidates. As I approached, I strained to catch the eye of the woman who appeared to be in charge: tall, with a statuesque bearing, her short hair only a little grayer around the face than the last time I'd seen her. Her smile was still gentle, working its way up to her eyes, even as her conversations with job candidates were brief and efficient. She appeared engrossed in conversation, so I attempted to wait patiently in line. *Thank goodness they sent her. I had forgotten that she'd been promoted and would be here. I was her homeroom student council rep. I made a 5 on the AP exam after taking her class, even if she didn't like the pun I slipped into that one report. I wonder if she remembers that nearly a decade later?*

"Hi, Julia! It's so good to see you!" I smiled confidently as I approached the table, noting the navy-blue tablecloth and the school crest on the banner draped across it. She cordially acknowledged me, though I suspected she had confused me with one of my sisters until I handed her my résumé. *One hundred percent cotton fiber paper, watermark facing the correct direction. First impressions count.*

"Sarah, how have you been? What have you been up to?" she said, the twinkle in her eye calming my nerves that had crept to the surface. In the ensuing conversation, I tried to indicate as clearly as possible without seeming desperate that I was eager to begin a career in secondary education. I dropped hints that I'd always been interested in teaching in independent schools, particularly Catholic ones, because I felt strongly about the mission-driven focus of such institutions. I would be graduating in May with a master's degree, I said, and I even let slip that I'd taken and passed the state's content exam for 6–12 English/Language Arts teaching certification.

"That's wonderful," Julia responded. A hair's breadth of a pause passed, and then she said, "But you don't have any experience. We're really looking for someone with experience this year. We'll keep your résumé on file, though. Be sure to stay in touch! It was wonderful to see you again." She had slid my résumé onto the table as she continued talking to me.

I hoped my smile looked genuine as I shook her hand. "You too. Have a great rest of your afternoon!" My steps were a little slower as I turned away. I looked confusedly down at the diagram of the hall before selecting another line of candidates to stand in.

Her words kept ringing in my ears. *You don't have any experience.* They stung more sharply each time they repeated themselves in my head. She knew me. She knew I was smart. She knew I was a hard worker. She knew I wasn't an athlete and therefore probably couldn't coach a sport, but she also knew I had been involved in enough other extracurriculars that I could moderate a club or chaperone dances.

The exchanges played out much the same way at each table I visited that afternoon. My graduation from a prestigious local independent school—even if a rival school—grabbed the attention of hiring committee representatives, as did my undergraduate alma mater and my almost-completed master's degree. My work experience suggested aptitude and experience that could transfer to "involvement in the extracurricular life of the school," as most of the job postings had phrased it. Once they realized the work experience didn't include time spent in the classroom, though, the facial expressions changed: a faint turn down at the corners of the mouth, a slight hardening of the gaze before a polite smile. "We'll keep your résumé on file," they all said. "But we're really looking for candidates who have experience. Good luck with your job search."

WHEN EXPERIENCE ISN'T ENOUGH

At first, I was flummoxed by the reactions I received from prospective employers. "Experience," it seemed, had a paradoxical, vague-yet-particular connotation. I had plenty of classroom experience by the time I neared the completion of my master's program, though it admittedly was as a student rather than as a teacher. And I did have teaching-adjacent experience (or so I thought) from working in a youth ministry office for more than two years: coordinating events, maintaining attendance and programming records, and interacting with the teens themselves on a weekly basis. All of these experiences correlated to the kind of work I had thought would be required of a classroom teacher. And yet, I discovered, it wasn't enough.

What I did have, though few of the people I met asked me about it, was subject-area experience. Often, "experience" in a job description appears in tandem with academic credentials or subject-area expertise, particularly for secondary education. Most often, holding a bachelor's degree in a field related to the subject one wants to teach demonstrates subject-area. For me, this component of "experience" was not an issue; I began my career search while in the final semester of my master's degree in English literature, and I held a PhD in English literature by the time a Catholic school hired me. I am, however, one of a dwindling number of individuals who choose to pursue degrees in the liberal arts-focused, college preparatory subjects taught in Catholic schools.

According to the American Academy of Arts and Sciences, bachelor's degrees awarded in the humanities have been declining since their zenith in the mid-twentieth century. While the number of undergraduate degrees awarded in education has outpaced subject-area humanities degrees for decades, they also have been steadily declining for much of the last fifteen years. In 2019–2020 (the most recent year for which data is available as of the time this book went to press), approximately 85,000 undergraduate degrees in education were awarded. This number represents a drop of more than 22,000 from the most recent high point in 2005–2006. Even so, more than twice as many degrees were awarded in education than in English or in liberal arts/general studies/ humanities in 2019–2020. Education degrees also outnumbered mathematics/statistics degrees by more than three to one, and religious studies/philosophy degrees and theology/ religious vocation degrees combined total a mere one-fourth of the education degrees awarded. This 10 percent share of bachelor's degrees awarded in the humanities represents the smallest such percentage since 1987. In the meantime, more than half of the degrees awarded were in the sciences and engineering (35 percent) and business (19 percent).

These trends in higher education have the potential to upset educational hiring practices, particularly for Catholic schools providing a liberal arts-based, college preparatory curriculum. If the number of people earning humanities degrees continues declining, then a shifting of priorities—or a broadening of "experience" considered while reviewing candidates—could help to match the vocation with the opportunity. With larger proportions of college graduates entering the workforce with subject-area expertise in the sciences and business, a renewal of emphasis on transferable skills may become necessary in order to fill positions in English, world languages, and theology departments. In addition, as the number of potential teacher candidates with readily apparent content area knowledge in liberal arts subject areas continues to dwindle, *enthusiasm* or *charism* for the subject area could count in lieu of relying solely on institutionally recognized "expertise."

THE "RIGHT" EXPERIENCE

After my first humbling foray into the world of independent and Catholic school job-seeking, I looked for ways to gain teaching experience. I had already decided not to pursue a PhD immediately after completing my master's degree, telling myself that having missed the testing and application deadlines would allow me more time to research schools and prepare my writing samples. I remained determined to keep my options open, the voice of one of my master's program mentors echoing in my head:

> *If you can get a tenure-track job, teaching in a college or university can be a great gig. That said, you have to go where the work is. If you can find a good secondary school gig, especially in an independent school that places less emphasis on teacher certification, you'll have a much more stable situation and probably make more money.*

In the meantime, I took the well-meant advice of peers and mentors. I filled out substitute teaching applications for archdiocesan schools, independent schools, and even some of the local public school systems. I submitted my cover letter and résumé to any local independent or Catholic school advertising high school English teacher openings. I trawled job boards through the summer looking for the rare-but-not-wholly-implausible late-summer job posting. And, as it became clear my chances of securing a high school teaching position for the upcoming school year were rapidly dwindling, I began applying for adjunct teaching positions at any local college within a reasonable driving distance of my house.

Two weeks before the start of fall semester, I got the call. A smaller school, touting itself as the liberal arts college within the state university system, had three sections of freshman composition needing an instructor. They wanted to meet with me in person.

I discussed my plans with the department chair, a silver-haired woman with a hint of a drawl and an enchanting, reassuring smile, before she offered me the position. The one-hundred-mile drive from my house to the college would be a trek, and the gas card offered to me barely covered a week's worth of driving. Still, the department chair promised me twice weekly classes that met back-to-back to reduce the driving I would have to do, and the position offered me a chance to gain the teaching experience I needed in order to get the job I wanted. I accepted, already anticipating the updates I would be able to make to my résumé before the next K–12 education hiring cycle.

In a different meeting space the following February, I stood outside the heavy wooden doors adjusting my suit jacket before walking into the room. I wore a different shirt this time, carefully selected to look flattering and distinctive but not ostentatious. My freshly printed résumés included my most recent adjunct teaching experience, and I could finally boast a list of professional references that included an actual educator—a professor and a department chair to boot. My cover letters now emphasized the transferability of the concrete teaching skills I had learned in the first-year teacher gauntlet. Since all the schools here were Catholic schools, too, I made sure my cover letter mentioned my alumna status and my "firm belief in the value of a Catholic education."

With a deep breath and a smile on the exhale (a trick I'd learned from a family portrait session as a tween), I crossed the threshold. The first table I spotted belonged to one of the high schools I'd talked to the year before, the representative the assistant principal I'd seen previously. I walked up confidently with my hand outstretched and the assistant principal's name on the tip of my tongue.

"Ah, yes! You're back," he said, before I could greet him. "So nothing worked out for you last year, huh?"

The silence lasted only a beat before I stammered, "No, not quite, but I'm looking forward to seeing what's available this year."

"Well, we don't have any English openings this year, but good luck!" he said as he turned to the young man who had sidled up during our conversation.

It's okay, I reassured myself as I walked away from the table. *You can do this.*

As my eyes scanned the array of tables and school banners, I saw Julia. With another deep breath-smile-exhale combination, I strode across the room while trying to shake off the nerves from my previous conversation. She betrayed no surprise at seeing me again as she smiled and asked, "It's so good to see you! What have you been up to since the last time we spoke?" I handed her my updated cover letter and résumé as I explained my position at the liberal arts college. I told her exactly what I'd rehearsed on the drive over: after a year in the college classroom, I had realized that college freshman composition courses occurred too late in the learning process for many students to try to remediate writing skills. As a result, I was even more committed to working with high school students.

"What experience do you have working with high schoolers?" she asked.

"Well, I've been working in a youth ministry office for two and a half years, and I've volunteered in youth ministry settings since I graduated from college." She nodded slowly as I spoke.

"That's wonderful to hear," she finally said. "But you don't have any high school English teaching experience. It's not at all the same thing as teaching college students." Before the pause became long enough to be awkward, she added, "We'll keep your résumé on file. Good luck with your job search, and stay in touch!"

"Will do," I managed to reply. "I hope the rest of your day goes well."

I can't win, I kept thinking to myself. The desperation began to rise at the back of my throat, a small metallic-tasting knot threatening eventual tears. *How am I supposed to get high school teaching experience if no one will hire me?*

THE TEACHING "EXPERIENCE" CONUNDRUM

The interactions I experienced at my second education job fair revealed a tension I would continue to encounter during my teaching career: the perceived incompatibility between secondary and postsecondary teaching experience. This tension is probably best explored in depth elsewhere, but it does highlight another facet of the "experience" independent and Catholic schools seek.

When job postings for teaching positions mention experience, the language may initially appear straightforward: "prior experience required," or "three to five years' experience preferred." Alternatively, the language may stipulate experience teaching a specific subject area or concentration without identifying a time frame or tenor, such as "prior experience teaching [subject] or [specific course] required." Sometimes, particularly in independent schools, a posting will acknowledge the myriad experiences that render potential teachers a good fit for the position. A recent job posting on the National Association of Independent Schools careers website, for example, notes "not every great teacher's path to teaching is a straight line." Regardless of the language and employers' best intentions, though, these descriptions intended to procure experienced teachers leave room for interpretation that risks discouraging potential educators.

Granted, the framing of these job postings presents little conflict for many prospective applicants. For the first-year Catholic school teachers entering the profession from bachelor's or master's programs in university education departments, the experience sought by employers often takes the form of a practicum or "student teaching" experience. During such a practicum, a teacher candidate is assigned to a classroom for a semester and has the opportunity to develop lesson plans and teach the class while under direct supervision of a veteran teacher. Teachers who transition into Catholic school positions after having worked in public schools or in independent elementary/secondary schools, meanwhile, bring with them experience from prior years of teaching in environments with an apparent similarity to the one they wish to enter.

For first-year Catholic school teachers who are "career transitioning" from anywhere other than an elementary or secondary school position, though, demonstrating "relevant" teaching experience becomes a much more challenging task. In fact, according to a 2017 survey by Phoenix University, 34 percent of K–12 classroom teachers are career changers or "second career teachers (SCT)." Of this group, 36 percent come from business and management careers. In addition, career changers are recognized by their educator peers as bringing key benefits to the classroom, including "'real world' applications […] fresh ideas, more teacher diversity, and unique teaching styles and perspectives on the material taught." Given these advantages offered by career changers, Catholic schools should consider the transferability of existing skills sets when ascertaining applicants' experience. If they already do so, taking an even more compassionate stance toward experience could be employed to schools' and prospective teachers' mutual benefit.

The significant shifts taking place in higher education, both in terms of the degrees earned and the careers pursued by graduates, eventually result in a pool of potential teachers who have more diverse credentials that ought to be acknowledged. Humanities degrees, for example, have long held their reputation as providers of the "soft skills" necessary for and readily transferable to multiple career fields. Of these skills, sources from Best Colleges to Indeed.com identify communication and critical thinking skills as the most valuable to humanities graduates. One result of these "transferable skills" is the movement of graduates with these degrees into corporate or other environments that might not provide opportunities for "classroom experience" but do offer chances to engage in corporate training, new hire mentorship, or philanthropic initiatives that give prospective teachers the "soft skills" needed to be successful in the Catholic school classroom.

WITNESS AND EXPERIENCE

Catholic schools have a duty to be responsible stewards of the financial resources to which they have access. One of the ways Catholic schools can do so is to balance the need for experienced teachers with the expenses that may result from ensuring these newly hired teachers have the training necessary to perform their jobs. The potential risk involved, however, is alienating potential job candidates who feel called to the teaching vocation but whose pedigrees might not meet first-glance expectations.

In these instances, incorporating "witness" into hiring processes can help to bridge the developing gap between education/teaching experience as traditionally conceived and candidates' transferable skills and experiences. Some of these steps are already being incorporated into job applications, but giving candidates' unique experiences additional consideration could be helpful. Asking teachers to provide supplemental information, whether in the form of a teaching philosophy statement or a testimonial regarding the candidate's discernment of a vocation in education, could allow potential teachers to articulate their understanding of the demands of education. Although it would result in more robust teaching dossiers, the additional information could allow more diversely qualified candidates to present themselves in a way that might be more positively received. In addition, incorporating sample lesson plans or teaching demonstrations as part of the face-to-face interview process could provide evidence of candidates' affinity for the charism of education.

In his letter to the Romans, St. Paul declares, "God doesn't call the qualified; he qualifies the called." Perhaps Catholic schools should too.

CHAPTER 4

CERTIFIABLY QUALIFIED

"Hi, Sarah. It's Simon, from the school you just interviewed with," the voice on the other end of the phone said. The butterflies in my stomach immediately went into overdrive. "I normally don't do this, but my assistant principal just walked into my office and said, 'You need to call this woman right now. She was our first interview, but we don't want to interview anyone else. We can't let her get away.' So, would you like to come work for us?"

After spending ten years searching for a teaching position in a Catholic school, the job offer I finally received felt shockingly—miraculously?—fast. In fact, I had been in the middle of a higher education job search after completing my PhD. I had spent most of the fall updating my online academic dossier and sending my application materials to any position I could find with even a tenuous connection to my teaching experience (nine years by then: three years at the college level and six at the high school level) or to my research interests (eighteenth century British literature, with a minor area concentration in early modern drama).

As winter segued into spring, I had only received two job offers from universities—one for an adjunct teaching position, the other for a one-year position that would triple the number of students I taught and cut my pay by 30 percent. Having never fully abandoned the possibility of remaining in K–12 education, I renewed my pursuit of a high school teaching position in a Catholic school. In some ways, this route made more sense; I was already in my sixth year of teaching high school students in an independent school, I had served as a club moderator for three years, and I had agreed to sit on a couple of committees. The email requesting an interview nevertheless surprised me, after so many noncommittal "we'll keep your résumé on file" and "we decided to hire one of our substitute teachers" responses. The interview itself surprised me further still: conducted via Skype in the days before online meetings and interviews became ubiquitous, the interviewers were friendly, the questions relevant to my own experiences.

Less than half an hour after my Skype meeting concluded, the phone rang.

Stunned and thrilled, I stammered a response that escapes me now and then asked for additional details regarding the position. He apologized for the salary amount; I didn't admit to him that what he offered was a significant raise from my salary at the time. After a few more exchanges regarding classroom experience and the likely courses I would be asked to teach (one in my graduate field of study and one I had taught since I started working with high school students), he concluded with, "And of course, you'll need to get certified. But we'll cover the cost of your certification courses."

Okay, I thought to myself. *That's no surprise. Certification was one of the requirements for the job. How bad could it be?*

TEACHER CERTIFICATION BASICS

Teacher certification is not a new phenomenon. Ever since the mid-nineteenth century education initiatives established what would eventually become the public school system in the United States, teacher preparation has been one of the issues at the heart of education policy. The New York University Steinhardt School of Culture, Education, and Human Development highlights the contributions of Horace Mann and other education reformers who advocated for a new model of teacher preparation. The goal of this new model was to transform education into a profession akin to the medical and legal professions. The first forays into formalized teacher preparation were the "normal schools" that provided subject area and pedagogical instruction. These schools eventually became state teacher colleges and, later, schools of education within state universities. Regardless of the organizational structure, higher education has provided much of the pedagogical training for K–12 classroom educators for the last several decades.

The specific requirements might vary among programs or from one state to another, but all teacher certification programs purport to have the same goal: to ensure teachers are "highly qualified" to work with their student populations. TEACH.org, a nonprofit organization founded by the US Department of Education, explains on its website how teacher certification programs help to ensure the quality of teachers in schools. First, programs often require the completion of coursework in pedagogical methods and educational trends. Would-be teachers must complete a series of subject-specific coursework, particularly those who wish to teach at the secondary level. In addition to the required coursework, teacher certification also involves the completion of a series of exams to demonstrate competence both in the prospective teacher's subject area and in pedagogical best practices. Occasionally, the "basic skills" assessments can be exempted through already holding an advanced degree, for example; however, most prospective teachers must complete these exams and submit their scores to a certifying agency in order to be eligible for a teaching certificate.

Finally, many teacher certification programs require the completion of field experiences. These field experiences often are a combination of visits the teacher candidate makes to schools and of student-teaching or practicum-based field experiences. In the first instance, visits to other schools allow prospective teachers to observe others in their field in order to witness best practices in action. In the case of student-teaching/practicum experiences, the teacher candidate is able to put into practice the pedagogical lessons learned through coursework and observation. The teacher candidate also benefits from being observed by a certified teacher who is able to provide feedback on the teacher candidate's lessons and classroom management skills.

On its face, the general requirements for teacher certification appear reasonable enough; teachers need to be familiar with their content area(s), they need to have an understanding of pedagogical best practices, particularly for the age group(s) they will teach, and they need to demonstrate their mastery of these skills through objective and hands-on assessments. The emphasis on quality education as outlined in legislation like ESSA has lent additional impetus to ensuring that meeting these basic components of teaching certification responds to the changing needs of both students and prospective educators. Further inspection, however, reveals the latent rigidity of these requirements in practice and the challenges they pose—particularly for teachers in independent and Catholic schools.

"BUT YOU HAVE A PHD"

Once hired, the discussions about enrollment in a teacher certification program didn't begin until after I had a semester of teaching under my belt. I learned there were two options: a certification-granting master's degree program and an alternative pathway to certification program. For teachers holding a bachelor's degree, the graduate degree program had the additional benefit of moving them into a higher pay scale (since education factors into determining compensation).

"But you have a PhD," the new principal said to me in her office one afternoon. "So there's not much advantage to doing the master's program."

"No," I agreed. "I'm not interested in a second master's degree."

"The thing is," she continued, "what I've heard from our teachers who've completed the alternative certification program is that it's an awful lot of work. Lots of forms to complete, lots of boxes to check—seemingly more than with the master's degree. I know you're capable of completing the work; that's not the issue. In fact, I'm sure with your PhD, it won't even be that difficult, but I hear it feels a lot like busy work, and I don't want you to feel like you're wasting your time."

"Okay. What's the cost difference?" I asked.

"Well, we'll cover the alternative certification program at 100 percent. We'll cover 50 percent of the cost of the master's program," she said.

"Oh, really?" I said, remembering my conversation from the previous spring. *That distinction didn't come up when I accepted the job*, I thought. *I thought the costs would be covered—full stop. Maybe I should've asked more questions.* "May I have a few days to think it over before I give you my answer?"

"Sure! Of course," she said. "The application deadline for the alternative certification program isn't for another few weeks, so we have a little bit of time still." She rose and began to come around her desk, reaching for the office door as she did so. "Thanks so much for stopping by, Sarah. I hope to get into your classroom soon. I'm hearing great things!" I smiled in return, clutching my clipboard to my chest as I slipped past her into the hallway.

A VIABLE ALTERNATIVE(-PREPARATION PROGRAM)

After my conversation with the principal, I did my own research into both of the options she had presented. I also asked a local university about taking only the certification-specific courses required by the state and allowing my graduate school coursework to fulfill the remainder of the requirements. In the end, I opted for the alternative-preparation program offered through a regional state-approved agency. The Education Commission of the States and other organizations note alternative pathways to certification have been on the rise since the 1980s, when New Jersey was the first state to adopt such a program. Originally, these programs were developed as a way to address falling enrollment in traditional teacher education/certification programs and the growing need for teachers. Tailored for prospective teachers who have not yet completed a traditional program, alternative-preparation programs are considered ideal for those who want to transition into teaching from another career or for those who hold advanced degrees in a content area but have not fulfilled all of a state's certification requirements.

Opinions vary somewhat among the professional education community about the effectiveness of alternative-preparation programs. Although they continue to see rising enrollment numbers, these increases do not necessarily translate to higher numbers of students completing the programs. The Center for American Progress's 2022 update to its report on the alternative teacher certification sector notes a net drop in the number of students completing such alternative-preparation programs. Moreover, the report highlights areas for further research. One area is how teachers certified through alternative-preparation programs compare to their traditionally prepared peers in terms of providing quality instruction. Another is the small but growing body of research suggesting that alternative-preparation program graduates are more likely to leave the teaching profession.

In spite of these trends and questions, my decision ultimately came down to two factors: my employer's willingness to cover 100 percent of the costs associated with the alternative-preparation program and the fact that an additional master's degree would not substantially change my compensation package. When my colleagues heard I had enrolled in a teacher certification program, their first reaction was rarely, "But why aren't you certified? Haven't you been teaching for years already?" Instead, I most often heard something along the lines of, "But that's ridiculous. You have a PhD!"

The comments seemed to suppose that because I had completed a terminal degree in my subject area, I should know enough to be able to teach. However, many PhD programs (particularly those at large research universities) often focus most of their program requirements on training future researchers rather than successful teachers. Even though my particular program afforded students many opportunities to develop and teach classes themselves while completing their coursework and dissertations, not all PhD programs do so. As such, the indignant solidarity behind the exclamations of, "But you have a PhD!" fell a little flat for me, even as I appreciated the sympathy.

"WHERE DO YOU TEACH?"/"I'M SORRY YOU HAVE TO GO THROUGH THIS"

One of the things I did find frustrating after beginning the alternative-preparation program was my seeming "outsider" status as a teacher in a Catholic school. The difference became apparent from the moment I set foot in my first seminar.

Our cohort was one of the larger ones to have enrolled in recent years. My cohort-mates were friendly, coming from a myriad of life and previous work experiences. Since our cohort's size exceeded the seating capacity for any one of the class meetings by a good measure, class rosters often varied from course to course. The common refrain of "Where do you teach?" echoed throughout the classroom at the beginning of most sessions.

"I teach at Such-and-Such," would come a response.

"Oh! Is that part of the city or the county system?"

"City," the first teacher would say before segueing into a discussion of local school boards, system superintendents, and the reorganization of school clusters as populations shifted.

"What about you?" they eventually would turn to me and ask. When I would tell them, awkward pauses were often my only reply before a vague, "Oh, yeah... I think I've heard of it."

I received the same reactions from several of the instructors, who did their best to hide surprise behind smiles and small talk. When a course required the completion of an assignment that needed state testing data (something my school didn't participate in), my instructions were often either to "make do" with a facsimile that I could manipulate to fit the requirements of the assignment or to use another school's data. My assignments occasionally received penalties for not containing information about my school that my school couldn't provide because the information didn't exist. The instructors were well-meaning and were trying to work with me, I could tell, but I could also see the confusion in their eyes as they tried to figure out someone who didn't quite fit.

I also struggled with the reminders that my prior educational experience, including the observation records from employers and the letters of recommendation I had procured as part of my job search, were not considered sufficient demonstration of content-area or pedagogical mastery to be eligible for teacher certification. The alternative-preparation program I enrolled in required the completion of two observations by an appointed supervisor that were scored in all evaluation areas at the level of "Proficient" or "Exceptional." After my first two such observations met the "Proficient"/"Exceptional" level in all observation criteria, I asked the program director about the possibility of early program completion if all other coursework and portfolio materials had also been completed.

"No," she said. "You still have to complete all eight required observations."

My principal and my program-appointed supervisor were sympathetic. The supervisor, who did observe my teaching the mandatory eight times over two years, was good-natured as we held our required post-observation debrief meetings. Her comments of, "Well, you're already such a strong teacher," and "You know your students and your content admirably well," always pleased and comforted me—as if she also recognized the uniqueness of my position within the program. My principal was more direct. When we would meet about my program progress, she would say, "I'm sorry you have to go through this." She often mentioned my prior teaching experience as she lamented the state certification agency's inflexibility regarding programming requirements. Because none of my ten years in the classroom had taken place in my current state or as part of a teacher preparation/certification program, none of them "counted" in the state certification agency's eyes. I was, to them, no different than a first-year teacher.

THE EXPERIENCE/CERTIFICATION PARADOX

Eventually, I learned that my frustrations with pursuing teacher certification were not unique.

The first person to speak to me about it, Harold, sat next to me during several of our certification program seminars. Harold had moved to the area after spending years as a vice provost at a small university in another state, and his research had included work on education policies in our state (among several others). Looking to make a career change and influence young people's education in a more direct way, he found a paraprofessional job in a public school system that did not require certification as a prerequisite for employment. When I asked him what prompted his decision to pursue state certification, Harold told me that after observing some of the policies in the school where he worked, he scheduled a meeting with administration to make some suggestions. The administrators, after hearing his feedback, replied, "Well, that's all well and good, but you don't know what you're talking about. You're not certified."

Where Harold had seen this comment as motivation to acquire the certification that seemed to be the only currency for a seat at the policy table, my colleague Agnes's friend became discouraged to the point of seeking employment elsewhere. This friend was a board-certified MD who desired a career change and wanted to work with young people, so she applied for a job teaching high school biology and anatomy. She had a wealth of practical experience that could enliven the classroom and a working knowledge of the material she would be teaching. And yet, certification became a seemingly insurmountable hurdle because her undergraduate degree was not in the subject area she would be teaching.

Later, Irene agreed to discuss her own journey toward teaching certification with me. An educator with fifteen years of classroom experience in English and language arts, she had earned an undergraduate degree in literature in a foreign language. Although she had pursued graduate studies in comparative literature, unforeseen circumstances had prevented her from completing the degree. Still, she had taught secondary English courses for more than a decade by the time we became colleagues. Once she began exploring the teaching certification process, though, she realized that the specificity of her bachelor's degree not only limited the fields in which she could potentially pursue teaching certification, her graduate coursework was not sufficient on its own to qualify her for a teaching certificate in secondary English.

The more stories I heard, the more disconcerted rather than comforted I became. *There has to be another way,* I thought. *We can't risk losing good people like this.*

WITNESS AND CERTIFICATION

Teacher certification programs, designed to certify public school teachers, struggle to engage in meaningful ways with schools and teachers who are working with different mindsets and in different settings. As a result, the teacher certification process poses several stumbling blocks for private school teachers generally and Catholic school teachers specifically.

The first of these challenges stems from the shortcomings of a one-size-fits-all approach. From the vocabulary used during the coursework to the reporting required as part of the assessment process, the programs seem primarily focused on encouraging all teachers to approach their profession in the same way. For those teachers who work in other settings, the challenge lies in trying to find the relevant connections to their professional experiences. Catholic school teachers in particular find themselves having to complete teacher education/certification programs that cannot teach—or assess—the explicitly Catholic content area knowledge and pedagogical best practices needed for their professional development.

The second of these challenges is an outgrowth of the value of experience first mentioned in the previous chapter. To meet this challenge, schools should bear witness to the depth and breadth of prospective teachers' experiences. Within this context, "witness" could encompass an observation framework that takes place prior to requiring enrollment in a teacher certification program. Similarly, "witness" can and should involve some type of mentorship or supervisory program; these mentors and supervisors could provide targeted facilitation of coursework completion in areas identified by the initial observation process as areas of growth. Implementation of such a program could be possible within a Title II-eligible framework, if that remains a priority for Catholic schools and school systems wishing to maintain a certification requirement.

It is time to envision a new, Catholic approach to vetting and preparing teachers for the Catholic school classroom. Bearing witness to teachers' expertise and experiences while meeting their specific needs as Catholic educators in Catholic schools is integral to embracing the intersections of culture, education, and faith.

CHAPTER 5

PROFESSIONAL FORMATION

With my eyes closed, the little sounds of the auditorium came to life: the hum of the HVAC system, the squeak of a folding chair hinge as a colleague shifted in his seat three rows behind me, the rustle of a cough drop wrapper several feet to my right.

"This first time," the woman at the podium onstage crooned, "I want you simply to listen to the words. Let them wash over you. After I finish, I'll read it again, and I'll give you additional instructions before I do so."

I settled deeper into my chair and sighed contentedly as I prepared to listen to the Bible passage that had been selected for the meditation exercise. *This is it,* I thought. *This is what I've been waiting for.*

In high school, I loved the opportunity retreats offered to step away from my day-to-day life—the classes, the homework, the extracurriculars, the petty dramas ubiquitous to high school students. I secretly looked forward to them, even if I occasionally tried to adopt a casual nonchalance about going. I enjoyed the anticipation of traveling to a retreat house outside of town and the camaraderie formed during the road trip. My heart often thrilled a little as our bus rounded the final corner, bringing the modest retreat house into view across tall, gently waving grass. Granted, I groaned a little through the icebreaker activities often used to kick off the retreat, but I was in my element once we began the schedule of talks and small-group discussions. The cliques became less rigid; people I rarely spoke to in the hallways at school became confidants (or at least friendly) over the course of the weekend.

Most of all, though, I remember the highlights of our retreats: the guided meditations and the worship that often occurred on the final night. I immersed myself fully in these experiences, always coming away from them with a new and compelling spiritual connection. I followed the meditation prompts given by the retreat leader as I lay on my back in a large meeting space with dozens of other teens; the vivid images that came to mind during those sessions are still with me today. A lump would often rise to the back of my throat while praying, the candlelight making everything in the room glow. Peace, love, awe, and wonder swirled within me in these moments, and I never wanted them to end.

Remembering my experiences on retreat in high school, I was thrilled when I joined a Catholic school and learned that an all-day faculty retreat occurred each year, usually falling the day after our prospective student open house. Rather than the awe-inspiring experiences I clung to from my youth, however, the day seemed somewhat perfunctory. A few times, we did meet somewhere off-campus, but I found myself irritated rather than excited by the drive to an unfamiliar location. The talks focused on our roles as teachers, leaving me feeling constrained by the limits of one component of my identity. The small-group discussions felt a little short, somewhat superficial, and fumblingly awkward, perhaps exacerbated by the lack of icebreakers I had bemoaned in my youth. The small service project that rounded out our half day, though energizing after sitting through the morning's talks, limited fellowship opportunities. Although we celebrated Mass together, until the guided meditation session in the auditorium several years into my Catholic school tenure, I often came away from faculty retreat days disappointed and unfulfilled.

RETREAT MODELS: OPPORTUNITIES AND CHALLENGES

Many opportunities and models exist for Catholic school faculty retreats, from off-site locations and programming to travelling retreat facilitators to guides for schools to build and facilitate their own retreat experiences. Retreat centers like Mercy Center Auburn in California and Holy Family Passionist Retreat Center in Connecticut offer facilities and programming specifically geared toward Catholic school faculty, whether on an individual or whole-faculty basis. Other organizations such as the Sophia Institute for Teachers offer on-site and virtual retreat options for Catholic school faculty. Alternatively, individual schools and districts such as the Toronto Catholic District School Board have developed their own planning guide for staff retreats. Whatever the format, the goal of a faculty retreat remains the same: as the Toronto

Catholic District School Board says, "Retreat experiences invite the community to nurture the spirit within so that the spirit of the community may more credibly radiate the presence of the One in whose name we exist."

In retrospect, part of the disappointment I experienced after my first few faculty retreats may have stemmed from the stress and anxiety elsewhere in my life I had brought with me to the retreat setting. Even accounting for such a phenomenon, however, my retreat experiences revealed to me that some of the things I found most frustrating are similar to some of the letdowns from my high school retreat experiences:

They were "one-off" experiences. Much like most of the retreats I attended as a high school student, the faculty retreat often operated like a stand-alone event. In fact, some years, the only spiritual component of the day was Mass at the beginning of the day; afterward, a service project would comprise the entirety of the remaining programming. Whatever the agenda, though, the faculty retreats often appeared set apart from the rest of our professional days, but not in the way the retreats I remembered from high school offered an opportunity to "step away" from the quotidian rigamarole. Instead, they felt out of step with our (or at least my) spiritual needs.

They were single-day events. Although most of my high school retreats lasted a full weekend, a few of them were only one-day events. The shorter the experience, I found, the less fulfilling the experience. Without sufficient time to get to know the members of one's small group for discussions or move gradually into deeper levels of conversation, the fellowship component of the retreats became somewhat limited. One of the things I loved most as a teenager was the opportunity to forge a "retreat bond" with people outside of my own circle of friends; the superficiality of acquaintanceship that persists in shorter retreats hampers rather than fosters spiritual solidarity, even when the participants are colleagues and interact with each other regularly.

There was little follow-up afterward. Occasionally, small groups on retreat would forge a bond so strong they would continue to hang out with each other well beyond the retreat weekend. Much of the time, though, the "retreat high"—the sensations of joy, peace, and connection with fellow retreatants—would fade after a few days, and life would resume its usual tenor and color as daily routines supplanted the rhythms of retreat life. On a faculty retreat, the combination of the one-off single-day elements lends itself to a fleeting "retreat high" (if one manifests at all) and a temptation not to return to the topics discussed or insights gained during the retreat once daily instructional duties reclaim our time.

Both the high school and the faculty retreats I have attended were planned by people—friends, trusted adults, and colleagues—who have good intentions for the experiences, and I am grateful for the work they have done over the decades. And there does seem to be an inherent "specialness" to a retreat that is always intended to feel distinct from the day-to-day experiences of the retreatants. Nevertheless, there remains a lot of potential to explore as far as the benefits to faculty and, in turn, to the students and school community.

PROFESSIONAL FORMATION: A "NEW" PHENOMENON?

A cursory internet search for "faculty formation" yields scores of search results, many of which are specific to Catholic schools and universities. These search results often refer to the necessity of ensuring all faculty, not just theology and religion department faculty, are familiar with the teachings of the Catholic Church so as to support those teachings through classroom instruction and interactions with students. Various documents written by the Vatican's Congregation for Catholic Education lay out this message as well, including *Lay Catholics: Witnesses to Faith* (1982):

> *The need for religious formation is related to this specific awareness that is being asked of lay Catholics [the awareness that what they are doing is exercising a vocation rather than merely participating in a profession]; religious formation must be broadened and be kept up to date, on the same level as, and in harmony with, human formation as a whole. Lay Catholics need to be keenly aware of the need for this kind of religious formation; it is not only the exercise of an apostolate that depends on it, but even an appropriate professional competence, especially when the competence is in the field of education. [...] What is at stake is so essential that simply to become aware of it should be a major stimulus toward putting forth the effort needed: to acquire whatever may have been lacking in formation, and to maintain at an adequate level all that has been already acquired.*

When it comes to the staffing of Catholic schools, though, the message of the Congregation for Catholic Education must extend to all faculty. According to the National Catholic Educational Association, 15.6 percent of all full- and part-time faculty and professional staff in Catholic schools during the 2020–2021 school year identified as non-Catholic. Another 6.3 percent of full- and part-time faculty and professional staff did not report their religious background. The *Journal for Catholic Education* has reported on these trends, too, noting "it remains important to consider their needs regarding their formation to accomplish this task [of supporting the universal mission of Catholic education]." Given these numbers, it becomes even more vital to ensure that Catholic faculty members understand their purpose and feel comfortable integrating their subject areas with the tenets of the faith undergirding the mission of the Catholic school.

In action, these goals appear to be achieved in a number of different ways, often specific to the needs of a particular school or diocese. For those schools falling under the aegis of a particular religious order—the Jesuits, for example, or the Marists—professional formation includes developing a familiarity with the charism of the religious order. At St. Ignatius High School in Cleveland, Ohio, for example, "All Saint Ignatius employees participate in a five-year faith formation program, structured to introduce them to our mission and identity as a Jesuit school." Marist High School in Chicago, Illinois, offers its faculty members "the opportunity to participate in the Marist Brothers's Evangelization Program" so they can "learn about the greater Marist mission and community" alongside employees from other Marist schools nationwide.

Diocesan Catholic schools also have similar programs, though these requirements seem to be framed somewhat more broadly. The Archdiocese of Los Angeles, for example, indicates in its administrative handbook that "it is the responsibility of the principal to provide faculty members with adequate opportunities for religious formation and an understanding of Church teaching" in order "to assure that teachers in a Catholic school become familiar with the purpose and philosophy of Catholic education, a basic theology of Catholic ministry, and the charism, mission, and history of the school in which they teach." The archdiocese also provides a four-year cycle of topics focused on Catholic formation and instruction to be implemented for all high school teachers.

It becomes apparent, then, that Catholic schools recognize the need to professional formation in keeping with Church directives and in light of their mission. It also becomes apparent that a wide variety of interpretations exist regarding how best to approach this vital component of building a Catholic faculty. What can such formation look like in its implementation?

PROFESSIONAL FORMATION: AN ONGOING PROCESS

The article "an" used by the Archdiocese of Los Angeles highlights what Ronald Fussell has identified as a potential shortcoming in some current models of professional formation. Currently a professor at Creighton University, Fussell previously worked as a Catholic school administrator in New Hampshire and a member of accreditation teams for other schools. Often, he focused on professional development during accreditation team school visits. One of his key takeaways from these visits was that professional development incorporated a myriad of approaches, from entirely individual- or teacher-focused models to entirely whole faculty- or school-focused models.

Because a Catholic school's mission and identity "is the lens through which teachers make day-to-day decisions, develop classroom policy, and encounter students in relationships of love and grace," according to Fussell, Catholic schools need to ensure their teachers are prepared to do so. While potential strength can be found in the ability to attune a professional development program to the specific needs of a school's faculty, Fussell did find one constant: that "Catholic schools will usually separate professional learning from faculty spiritual formation." This model, particularly when it limits discussion of Catholic identity and professional formation to a single experience, "sends a powerful negative message—that the same thing can happen in the classrooms." What is needed, therefore, are ongoing models that can keep faculty fully engaged with their formation in light of Catholic teaching while also giving them the confidence to take their insights into the classroom.

One such model to implement more widely would be making funds available specifically for retreat- and faith-focused individual professional formation. Felicity, who has spent her teaching career in both independent and diocesan Catholic schools, discussed the merits of such an approach with me. At one of her earlier employers, all faculty members were allotted funds to use in this way; in addition, the funds stayed with the teacher and rolled over from one year to the next as part of their compensation package. Since faculty members could choose for themselves how to use these funds, many faculty members would take the opportunity to travel to monasteries or other retreat sites for formal, week- or weekend-long retreat experiences. Other teachers might choose to allocate their funds for a single-day experience. Providing this degree of flexibility acknowledges the unique spiritual needs and personal schedules of individual faculty members while also making clear that individual formation is a vital component of one's development as a Catholic school teacher.

Another adoptable model would involve devoting regular faculty meetings to professional formation. This model would operate something like the youth group model many Catholic school students and alumni would find familiar: a talk or a video presentation could be presented to the whole group, followed by the opportunity for small-group discussions in order to process the material and lessons being presented. Such programming could still be focused on the particular needs of the Catholic school's faculty, but it also would reinforce the unity of purpose of the Catholic school's faculty. Moreover, building these sessions into the regular schedule of faculty meetings would address the limitations of the "one-off" faculty formation experience, instead supplementing such experiences with opportunities for extension and follow-up.

Regardless of the exact implementation, though, "because faith is dynamic and varies from person to person, leaders need to be intentional about building relationships to better understand the nature of educators' personal faith. Leaders make a strong statement about the relevance of faith formation to educators' lives when they are strategic about connecting opportunities for faith formation with educators' faith lives outside the school." This kind of integration of faculty members' lives—of their cultural and faith experiences that should inform their work as educators—is at the heart of witness and professional formation.

WITNESS AND PROFESSIONAL FORMATION

Whether part of an individual- or teacher-focused model or a whole-faculty model, witness should be an integral component of Catholic faculty professional formation. Combining individual faith and professional formation with on-campus opportunities to share retreat experiences with colleagues would tap into Fussell's call for sharing professional formation as a community. The small-group discussion component of a whole-faculty model would also provide faculty members the opportunity to witness to each other through sharing their experiences and processing the talk or video presented.

In addition to these two opportunities, forming faculty small groups to meet regularly could be a vibrant form of witness among faculty members. Such an approach would combine the strengths of the retreat-model small groups I enjoyed so much during high school with a peer-to-peer professional development model that whole-faculty professional development programming occasionally overlooks. While requiring faculty to join a small group could initially hamper the forging of relationships among faculty members (particularly if the method used to create the groups appears "forced"), giving faculty an opportunity to choose their meeting locations or even their meeting times, in addition to choosing the specific faith-related topics discussed during these meetings, could increase the "buy-in" and lead to professional formation at once authentic and in keeping with the spirit of Catholic education—forming of the whole person, whether faculty, staff, or student.

Even if Catholic schools cannot use government-provided funds to meet the spiritual needs of its faculty, these schools must make this type of faith-focused professional development an ongoing priority. There can still be something "special" about a faculty retreat, provided it serves as part of a broader approach to the spiritual development of Catholic school faculty and staff. As Fussell notes, professional formation "deemphasizes the utilitarian dimension of what [Catholic school educators] do, and instead focuses on holistic potential." His recommendation to connect the focus on Catholic identity at the heart of professional formation with the pedagogical focus of much professional development is explored further in the next chapter.

Professional formation *is* professional development. We cannot, as Catholic educators, separate the two.

CHAPTER 6

WHERE FORMATION MEETS FUNCTION

"Hi there!" Lydia walked into the darkened classroom and set her things down on a nearby desk.

I winked at Irene before replying, "Hey! What's going on?" We had deliberately kept the lights off in an attempt to avoid distractions from well-meaning colleagues, but our efforts had been mostly unsuccessful. In fact, Lydia was the second person to cross the threshold in the past half hour.

"Not much," Lydia answered. "I just finished up in another meeting and was walking back to the office. How about you?"

"We're working on summer reading book rationales," I said.

"Yeah," Lydia jumped in before I could continue. "What is this whole 'Catholic Identity' requirement about? Why are we being asked to do this so close to the end of the school year?"

Irene and I exchanged glances. "Well," I began, "I think it's part of a larger effort to ensure that the 'Catholic' in Catholic schools is present. It's not intended to be punitive, I don't think."

"Exactly," Irene continued. "And these documents aren't for us. They're intended to be a reference point in case someone asks why we chose a particular book, so that admin doesn't have to contact you over the summer to explain the choice."

"But why all of a sudden do they care about whether or not the book is 'Catholic' enough?" Lydia asked. "I mean, why now, on top of everything else we've dealt with this year?"

"I don't think it's about whether or not a book is 'Catholic enough,'" I replied. "It's about making sure we've thought about how the books we teach can be put into conversation with the Catholic faith—how we're considering what we're reading in light of how it can help our students understand their faith better." I had begun fidgeting with my Chromebook's browser by this point, trying to figure out how best to diffuse the situation. *There has been so much drama already this year,* I prayed. *Please don't let this spiral too.*

"Why is that our job, though?" Lydia pressed. "Isn't that the theology department's job? Why are we being asked to do their work?"

"But I don't think it's just the theology department's job," Irene chimed in. "If we're a Catholic school, so the thinking goes, then everything we do—both inside and outside the classroom—should be viewed through the lens of trying to understand the faith better."

"I think that's part of the reason why we're going to have these Catholic Identity Coaches next year, to help us figure out some of that integration," I added.

Lydia's tension was palpable at this point. "Well, if that's what they wanted me to do, then why did they hire me? Why, after five years here, am I just now hearing about this? I'm not Catholic; I don't understand these things. I mean, I'm glad I can come to you," she said, turning to me. "I enjoy the conversations we have about this stuff, but it's a lot to take in."

Irene and I exchanged another look. *Why indeed?* our eyes seemed to say to each other. "I enjoy talking to you about it, and I'm happy to keep doing it if you like," I said tentatively.

"And I'm happy to help too," Irene added. "I know it can seem like a lot, but it's not as daunting as it sounds."

"I know," Lydia said. "I'm just super stressed about having to do this on such a short turnaround."

"It'll be okay," I reassured her. "In the meantime, I can pull up some reference points to Church teachings that you can put in your own rationales. In fact, you can use my draft rationale if you like. I'll share it with you right now."

"Thanks so much! Y'all are the best." Lydia smiled genuinely, her eyes back to their customary sparkle. "See y'all back in the office," she said, picking up her planner and Chromebook and turning for the door.

"See ya!" Irene and I called after her.

Isn't that the theology department's job? If that's what they wanted, why did they hire me?

Lydia's words echoed through my head as her voice trailed off down the hallway. The questions she had asked were good ones, and I myself had wondered about them on more than one occasion. The longer I had taught at the school, the louder the question at the back of my mind had become: What does it mean to be a "Catholic" faculty?

DEMOGRAPHICS AND DENOMINATIONS

Many Catholic schools have grappled with this question, particularly during the last half century or so. The data provided by organizations such as the National Catholic Educational Association and the Pew Research Center seemingly paint a grim picture. We've already discussed the numbers themselves in previous chapters, but the trends bear mentioning again here.

Bishop Robert Barron, auxiliary bishop for the Archdiocese of Los Angeles and founder of Word on Fire ministries, has referred to this phenomenon as the "Nuns and Nones." The precipitous decline in discerned vocations to the religious life (the "Nuns," although many priestly orders have an educational focus) since the 1960s has greatly reduced the number of teachers and administrators who hail from the clergy and religious life. At the same time, the number of people in the broader population who prefer not to identify with a particular religious tradition or who might describe themselves as "spiritual but not religious" (the "Nones") has steadily increased, a phenomenon at least partly reflected in recent demographic studies of Catholic faculties.

Brian Sanchez, writing for *America* magazine in 2018, brought attention to the changing demographics of Catholic schools and the ways faculty can adapt to those changes. On one hand, as experts he interviewed point out, "The literature is abundant. Teacher diversity enhances participation, self-esteem, affirmation of particular values; it helps to reduce biases such as racism and discrimination, and it improves [student test] scores, among other benefits." Meanwhile, administrators such as Monsignor Aidan Carroll explain, "Our first concern is always that the person has the skills and preparation for a particular position," and diversity often follows from that primary concern. Although Sanchez and others often are referring to racial and ethnic diversity in these contexts, the "Nuns and Nones" phenomenon adds another layer to such discussions.

The changing perspectives of families considering Catholic education for their children raise the possibility that Catholic school faculty might be able to reach more students if they can "see themselves" in their teachers—in all ways. However, if schools were to consider this possibility, they nevertheless must still be intentional in their recruiting and formation of a faculty willing and able to support the Catholic identity of the school. So what, then, are Catholic schools to do?

"BOX-CHECKING" VERSUS "CHARISM"

One of the central conundrums surrounding this question begins with faculty hiring. Irene, whose career in Catholic education includes serving as a department chair for an upper school English department, has experienced what she refers to as "two ends of the spectrum." On one end of the spectrum, schools hire faculty who profess their Catholic identity in a specific, potentially narrowly defined way at the expense of subject-area expertise and/or rapport with young people. On the other end, schools hire faculty who possess admirable subject-area expertise and rapport with young people at the expense of determining whether or not prospective faculty members are prepared to support a Catholic school's mission and ethos.

In the former instance, she says, the result is that the perceived rigidity of acceptable faith expression within a school suggests intolerance of otherwise perfectly acceptable charisms within the Catholic church while also failing to meet the subject-specific educational needs of the students. In the latter instance, by contrast, the result often is a faculty long on subject-specific enthusiasm and expertise but short on the ability to teach their respective subjects through the eyes of faith—and to encourage students to see their subjects through such eyes. In these cases, faith becomes relegated to the purview of the theology department and campus ministry. Academically, faith becomes a required sequence of courses to be taken in school, but not considered a "core" subject area for purposes of calculating GPAs and college application or scholarship credentials. Outside the classroom, faith becomes a series of required cocurricular programming for which attendance is mandatory but otherwise something to be endured rather than relished.

Jonah, another teacher with more than twenty years of experience in Catholic education, refers to this phenomenon as "checking the box" versus "checking for charism." As a former department chair himself, he is well aware of his school's requirement that at least 50 percent of the faculty in any given department be Catholic. "While I understand the importance of maintaining a Catholic presence on campus, particularly as the number of priests in our school's order continue to decline, I can tell you that more than once, we've had an outstanding candidate with the potential to transform our department, but the nod ultimately went to a less-engaging candidate, often a lackluster teacher, who had checked the 'Catholic box' on the application," he told me. What he wishes could be accounted for in the application process, he says, is "whether or not a candidate is willing to embrace the charism [the spiritual gifts or values] of the Catholic faith."

At a minimum, the potential and willingness to engage with integrating Catholicism into their daily teaching (beyond praying at the beginning or end of class, although such devotional practices certainly have an important place in the life of a Catholic school) would be helpful to determine during the interviewing of prospective faculty members. Ideally, faculty recruitment would look for candidates who are "passionate about their subjects *and* know a lot about it," as Bishop Robert Barron phrases it—in reference to both their academic subjects and their commitment to teaching in Catholic schools specifically. One way to do so might be to indicate, as some schools already do, that faculty members' job titles are "Teacher/Minister" rather than only "Teacher." This language would highlight the vital role that faculty members have in facilitating the academic and the spiritual development of the students in their charge.

FORMING A CATHOLIC FACULTY: WHAT NEXT?

The Catholic Church provides additional guidance regarding the goals for Catholic schools and faculty. Moreover, it is aware of the effects that social and cultural changes can have on Catholic schools. The 2014 document *Educating Today and Tomorrow: A Renewing Passion* acknowledges what Catholic schools and faculty can and should be:

> *Catholic schools must be run by individuals and teams who are inspired by the Gospel, who have been formed in Christian pedagogy, in tune with Catholic schools' educational project, and not by people who are prone to being seduced by fashionability, or by what can become an easier sell, to put it bluntly.*

The commitment and focus described by these criteria are both aspirational and practical. Preparation not only for discussing faith but also understanding how to integrate faith into instruction provided to students is vital for *all* Catholic school faculty—not merely the theology department and not only those faculty members who practice Catholicism. In addition, making sure that faculty members have the tools to embrace the intersections of culture, education, and faith without losing focus on Catholic charism is also a priority.

When it comes to putting this goal into practice, though, approaches and results differ. One example of ensuring that a Catholic faculty understands the creed and charism at the heart of the school is through an overarching program. Raphael, a teacher and administrator with more than fifteen years in Catholic education, explained to me the program he has helped to head at an independent Catholic school. Run by a religious order whose numbers have been in sharp decline, the school realized two decades ago that it needed to prepare for the day when there may be no more members of the religious order on campus on a day-to-day basis. Developing a comprehensive program that refers to "The Way" of the religious order has allowed faculty and staff to engage in sustained conversations about the many facets of the order's charism, while also allowing faculty to exchange ideas and witness about how to implement this ethos into the curricular, cocurricular, and extracurricular lives of the school.

While the discussions have been fruitful, Raphael admits that individual faculty members have "bought in" at different rates and with varying degrees of enthusiasm. Those longtime faculty members who joined the community prior to the development of the initiative in particular have seemed somewhat reticent to embrace this seeming shift in focus from when they first arrived on campus. When I asked Raphael about the challenge this reticence might present, he remained optimistic about the long-term success of their efforts even as he acknowledged that continued efforts to engage with them will require additional creative strategies.

In these moments of hesitation, how should a Catholic faculty proceed?

"HERE, I'LL SHOW YOU"

While reflecting on the conversation I had with Raphael, I remembered the second part of the interaction Irene and I had with Lydia. She came back into the classroom where we were still working a short time later.

"Okay," she said, balancing her opened Chromebook in her left hand while scribbling furiously with her stylus. "I took a look at that sample language you emailed to us a little while ago, and it looks great. Thanks so much for putting it together and sending it out."

"You're welcome! I'm glad it was helpful," I replied.

"Well, that's the thing—it all looks great, but I don't have any idea what these documents are that you're referring to. I want to make sure I know what I'm saying if I'm going to include these documents in my own rationales."

"Oh!" Irene chimed in. "We can definitely help you with that." She opened the template I had shared with the department and began scrolling through the documents I had listed: official Vatican communications, excerpts from the Catechism of the Catholic Church, and article- and book-length studies covering some of the prominent questions that arise in English classes.

"Like, for instance, what is this one?" Lydia asked, pointing to my favorite on the list. Irene and I exchanged another smile.

"Oh, that's a good one," I said, "Though I've only read commentaries on it. I tried to read the original, and I was totally lost after four pages. Then again, that was nearly fifteen years ago, so maybe I should try again."

"Really?" Lydia looked nervous.

Irene jumped in. "Oh, no, it's fine—here, I'll show you what it's about..."

By the time we'd finished summarizing the documents I'd listed, Lydia's face had completely relaxed. "This is great," she said. "Those all sound really cool. I might still need help, but this is a great start. Thank you so much, again!"

"You're welcome! I enjoy talking about these kinds of things. I hope I didn't blather on too much about it."

"No, no! It was great, really," Lydia said.

"But yeah, I think that's supposed to be the purpose of the Catholic Identity Coaches," I continued.

"Yeah," Irene added, "though I guess we'll find out more about that in the fall."

"Probably, yeah," Lydia said, closing her Chromebook and stretching as she stood up. "In the meantime, I'm off to update these documents. Have a good summer, if I don't see you again!"

"You too!" Irene and I said together.

Is this the key? I wondered. *Is helping each other understand the "what?" and the "why?" the way to keep the "Catholic" in Catholic schools?*

THE POWER OF RELATIONSHIP

Though I didn't know it at the time, the interpersonal approach that seemed to allay Lydia's concerns is at the heart of what Church documents and education researchers have identified as key to successful faculty formation. *Educating Today and Tomorrow: A Renewing Passion* declares:

> *Catholic schools and universities educate people, first and foremost, through the living context, i.e., the climate that both students and teachers establish in the environment where teaching and learning activities take place. This climate is pervaded [...] by the values that are lived out, by the quality of interpersonal relations between teachers and students and students amongst each other, by the care professors devote to student and local community needs, by the clear living testimony provided by teachers and educational institutions' entire staff.*

The "lived out values" in "interpersonal relations" also have been studied by experts such as Ronald Fussell. In his study on an interrelated framework for lay educator faith formation, Fussell identifies four areas that help develop faculty who can put their formation into action in the classroom. These four areas include "the educator's relationship to the Church, interconnected processes of prayerful reflection and personal encounter, formative experiences with the lives of students, and formation in service [to others]." Across all four of these areas is the role of *relationships.* Study respondents consistently mentioned relationships as foundational to their experience as Catholic educators. Whether structured or informal, with other faculty or with students, the ability to seek greater understanding of their purpose as Catholic educators and to put their understanding into action through encounter deepened their own relationships with their work.

In moments of reticence or hesitation, the relationships between members of a Catholic school community can be transformative. A colleague in Florida brought Fussell's study into stark relief for me. At one point early in her tenure, a student suggested to her that she check out the Rite of Christian Initiation for Adults (RCIA) informational sessions at his parish. Initially, she responded that she wasn't sure about it because she didn't want to be or sound disingenuous. As she said to him, "I'm already Christian... I'm not sure I would consider converting to Judaism if I had gotten a job at a Jewish school, for example." He said to her, "Yeah, but God didn't put you in a Jewish school. He brought you here, to a Catholic school. Maybe that's something to think about." Rather than brushing off the teenager's comments, the teacher used this personal encounter as an opportunity for prayerful reflection—and decided to attend the RCIA class after all. She eventually converted to Catholicism, crediting her conversion to the relationships she developed with her students. This kind of witness should be at the center of putting formation into practice.

WITNESS, FORMATION, AND FUNCTION

Both the Catholic Church and educational research are clear on the necessity of putting Catholic values or "charism" at the center of Catholic education. They also agree that when it comes to putting this priority into practice, exact methods are going to differ based on the particular needs of any given faculty or school. Regardless of the methods used or the specific demographic makeup, though, the impetus to help all faculty and staff understand what it means to be a Catholic faculty remains.

To be a Catholic faculty, ultimately, is to couple formation with function. As Kyle Pietrantonio, executive director of the Duc in Altum Schools Collaborative, said on the *Catholic School Matters* podcast, Catholic charism is "*not* just the theology department's job. They can take the lead and be the subject-area experts," but it should be part of everyone's focus. Moreover, it should be "infused" throughout the school, particularly in how students and faculty treat each other.

Pietrantonio's comments point to the heart of witness as it relates to formation and function. In this case, witness means moving beyond seeing subject-area expertise and pedagogical know-how as entirely separate from faith development. Rather, it focuses on the intersections of culture, education, and faith while understanding the "what?" and the "why?" behind Catholic charism. It makes those intersections clear through direct instruction and lived and shared experiences. And in order to do all of those things successfully, *relationships* are required.

CHAPTER 7

DISCIPLINED DISCIPLES

As I sat in my usual seat at the corner of my classroom conference table, the tension in my shoulders began to turn into knots. We had been sitting in our weekly Friday afternoon faculty meeting for close to an hour and a half, and much of the meeting had focused on discussing a student's proposal to abolish the school's dress code. My colleagues' lively exchanges about the merits of the dress code had started to splinter into side conversations as we all grew weary of the subject and of sitting for so long. I initially had tried to keep up with the conversation so that I could complete the meeting minutes, but I hadn't typed anything in more than a quarter of an hour.

In fact, I had struggled to stay engaged in the conversation for much of the meeting. At the start of the conversation, I had attempted to help my non-sectarian independent school colleagues understand that our school tacitly endorsed the theory behind uniforms despite actively eschewing their perceived constraints. Our school's athletic teams wore uniforms to compete; we wore school colors before big games; and, for a couple of years at least, we had T-shirts that were distributed to the entire school community for wearing on our service learning days. Rather than being an oppressive disciplinary apparatus, dress codes and uniforms offered a daily visual reminder of our unity of purpose rather than only on days when we needed to do so for a local newspaper's photo op. My comments were met with awkward silence before the conversation shifted to the restriction of personal expression that some believed lay at the heart of the dress code.

As the conversation continued to devolve, I turned to Seth who happened to be sitting just behind me. "All of these debates would be moot if we went to uniforms," I said quietly to him. I smiled as benignly as I could, though I suspect the tension was still visible.

Seth leaned forward, the set of his mouth firm as he looked at me. "We'll go to uniforms over my dead body," he said, and sat back in his chair. He resumed taking notes, eyes fixed squarely on the legal pad in his lap.

I stiffened, my cheeks burning. *If nothing else, the uniforms would come with a shorter list of potential infractions*, I thought. *Maybe then these meetings would actually end on time.*

CATHOLIC "ON THE OUTSIDE" SCHOOL DISCIPLINE

When I daydreamed about getting a job in a Catholic school, I thought teaching in one would be fundamentally the same as having been a student in one. I believed that my thirteen years in plaid meant I knew the environment: the kinds of students who could cross the threshold of my classroom, the school culture, and the academic and behavioral expectations I could have of my students. Even as I remembered the bitterness that rose at the back of my throat as my regulation-length skirt was measured while classmates with much shorter skirts escaped disciplinary scrutiny, I recognized that my alma mater did have clearly articulated behavioral expectations, clearly articulated consequences for failure to meet said expectations, and a (mostly, to my adolescent eyes) consistent application of said expectations and consequences.

In fact, my experiences with Catholic school discipline were altogether less accurate than the stereotypes that persist in the popular imagination. While my mother and grandmother might have had hands lightly rapped with rulers by nuns in full-length habits, no such corporal punishment occurred during my time as a Catholic school student. The few nuns who did teach me were kind and compassionate, not threatening. Discipline in my elementary school years consisted of losing recess privileges; "major" or repeat disciplinary infractions resulted in detention and suspensions. "Demerits" replaced lost recess by the time I got to high school, and "work detail" became an alternative to detentions. (A student who had demonstrated poor stewardship of school resources, for example, might have the option of picking up trash around campus for an hour after school rather than serving a Saturday detention.) Even so, the uniforms remained. The perceived threat of swift justice loomed overhead. The whispered stories about what happened to the students who left under mysterious circumstances kept those of us who remained in line. Seemingly, what I saw of the system worked.

Other institutions study and appropriate these readily visible indicators of a clearly defined approach to school discipline—uniforms, strict disciplinary codes, a "no nonsense" approach to behavioral expectations. As public school systems nationwide continued to discuss school reforms during the late 1990s and early 2000s, some educators hoped that borrowing from what they perceived to be Catholic schools' recipe for achievement and success would reap similar rewards for public and charter schools. Success Academy Charter Schools CEO Eva Moskowitz even quipped, "We're Catholic school[s] on the outside." As Robert Pondiscio explains in his book, *How the Other Half Learns*, this concept "encompasses the old-school uniforms, routines, and strict classroom management" often associated with Catholic schools, particularly in urban areas. Unfortunately, and as some of the "no excuses" charter schools that adopted this approach to student discipline have learned, "Catholic on the outside" isn't enough.

"NOT ANOTHER DRESS CODE MEETING"

I looked down at the faculty preplanning agenda I had printed out and tried to make sense of the charts listing small-group rotations and session schedules for the afternoon. My new colleagues brushed past me on either side, calling to each other and trying to catch up on each other's summers as they deftly navigated the still-unfamiliar hallways.

"Do you have any idea where we're supposed to go next?" I said, turning to Zachary. "For some reason, I'm having a hard time understanding this." I shuffled the papers and thrust them under his nose.

Zachary smiled good-naturedly. "I think we're supposed to go in here next," he replied, gesturing toward the door just ahead. "At any rate, so long as we make it to all the sessions before lunch time, I think we'll be good. These things always get a little wonky once everyone starts moving, but things always end up working out. Don't sweat it."

"Are you sure? I don't want to get in trouble for being in the wrong rotation or anything; I'm still new here, after all."

"Trust me. It'll be fine," he said, stepping aside to let me enter the classroom first.

I scanned the room for a seat that would make me as inconspicuous as possible. One toward the back of the room but surrounded by returning colleagues seemed to fit the bill. *Bingo.* I shuffled across the room, trying not to hit anyone with my tote bag or spill my coffee. *I totally should've put a lid on this.* Once I took my seat, I glanced up at the presentation cued on the projector. The words "Dress Code Updates and Discipline Infraction Reporting Protocol" appeared in a bold-faced, sans serif font against a stark white background.

I groaned inwardly. *At least this shouldn't take as long as the discussions I'm used to.*

Forty minutes later, our session was the last one to dismiss. We had only gotten through half of the presentation and had still run ten minutes longer than allotted. My hand had started cramping from all the notes I had taken. I had eventually given up, overwhelmed by the volume of information and reassured by the presenter that the information would be shared electronically.

CATHOLIC "ON THE INSIDE": THE KEY TO SUCCESSFUL DISCIPLINE

Even I had fallen prey to the "Catholic on the outside" myth, although my circumstances were a little bit different. I had assumed that the trappings of discipline I remembered from my own experiences as a Catholic school student spoke for themselves. Much like Seth's mission statement comment to me years earlier, he was right about uniforms and dress codes being like "cutting the grass"; they need regular tending in order to be effective, but they are not a magic bullet. Ultimately, what I had to learn was more profound: much like the sacraments of the Catholic church, the outward vestiges of discipline are indicative of a much deeper reality unique to Catholic schools.

According to Dr. Thomas Burnford, "Self-discipline, rather than the harsh caricatures of Catholic school discipline of yesteryears, is the goal and hallmark of Catholic school culture." Recent studies by organizations like the Thomas B. Fordham Institute have concluded that Catholic school students exhibit better self-discipline than their public school counterparts, which in turn affects both academic achievement and long-term social and cultural benefits such as increased levels of civic engagement and philanthropic endeavors. According to the *National Catholic Register*, numerous explanations exist for this phenomenon. Some Catholic school educators suggest that setting clear expectations within a respectful environment lies at the heart of fostering self-discipline;

others counter that dress codes for both students and faculty that reinforce an environment of mutual respect are the key to instilling self-discipline. Still others regard the Catholic identity of the school and the virtue formation that follows as the heart of any school disciplinary effort. Meanwhile, the inclusion of families as partners in education serves as the focus for building a school culture that fosters self-discipline.

Regardless of the exact formula, the key to success lies in the acknowledgment that discipline and structure serve as vehicles for encouraging students to lead virtuous lives. The purpose for leading virtuous lives in turn derives from something larger than individual achievement: the recognition of the inherent dignity of each student.

This understanding is vital for all parties to understand and articulate. Auxiliary bishop Joel Konzen, SM, of the Archdiocese of Atlanta, spent much of his career working in schools prior to his elevation to auxiliary bishop. During an interview with Nick Carrier for *The Best You* podcast, Bishop Konzen described one of the biggest learning experiences from his early tenure as principal of Marist School. The first year as a principal in a school is always a year of transition, but for Bishop Konzen, the transition included conflict with the oldest students at the school. Specifically, Bishop Konzen's close adherence to school policies and procedures, interpreted by some as a departure from recent memory, resulted in differences over "pretty basic stuff." When one of the student publications on campus published harsh, demeaning things about other students at the school, Bishop Konzen had to intervene. This encounter taught him that remaining firm in one's convictions regarding the best course of action, particularly when a Catholic anthropology grounds that course of action, can help administrators navigate difficult situations and make future exchanges go much more smoothly. While Bishop Konzen did not divulge the details of this encounter during the interview, what became clear was this former administrator's commitment to affirming the dignity of each student and fostering that same consideration among the students under his charge.

Even with this connection in mind, however, Catholic schools should consider how best to articulate this recognition to the school community at large. Daniel Lapsley and Katheryn Kelley have commented on this phenomenon in the course of their analysis of character-moral formation in Catholic schools. As they note, "it should not be assumed that the character-forming aspect of Catholic education can be carried by the Catholic identity of the school alone." Instead, they advocate for "an explicit, intentional, and visible pedagogy of moral, civic, and intellectual virtues." Perhaps one way to begin incorporating this kind of pedagogy is through the witness of discipline.

THE "LETTER" VERSUS "SPIRIT" TENSION

Early in my Catholic high school teaching career, a young man named Asher crossed the threshold of my classroom. His easy smile and good manners were both charming and disarming, and while not necessarily the strongest of my students, he seemed motivated to do well. He did, however, develop a curious habit of being absent on the day of a unit quiz or test—a phenomenon that resulted in having additional time to prepare based on the policies regarding making up assignments. In such circumstances, it was the student's responsibility to reach out to the teacher to schedule the make-up assignment. Moreover, the assignment had to be made up within an established time frame before disciplinary consequences including grading penalties and detentions would apply.

When Asher happened to miss the day of a test and did not follow up with me to schedule the make-up, I scheduled an appointment for him to make up the test in the school's testing center after school and communicated the details to him via email. He was a no-show for the appointment. While he did eventually sit for the make-up test, he did so outside of the permitted testing window; accordingly, I applied the late penalty to the test grade and initiated the detention paperwork.

I received a request to meet with the principal to discuss the matter a few days later.

"Hey there! Come on in and have a seat. Why don't you tell me what's going on with Asher," she said warmly. I clutched my clipboard in front of me as I smiled and stepped in to the small but cozy office.

I explained the sequence of events that had transpired over the previous two weeks: the absence on test day, the no-show for the initial make-up date, and the eventual make-up date outside of the window established by school policy. She nodded sympathetically throughout, then folded her hands together and took a deep breath.

"It sounds like you've taken all the right steps and followed the advice of your department chair and your mentor. Here's the thing, though..."

She went on to explain that Asher's father had been in treatment for a terminal illness for two years and that the prognosis wasn't good. The situation was kept in close confidence within the school community out of respect for the family, which explained why I hadn't yet heard about it. Because of his family's work schedules, Asher bore responsibility for driving his father to many of his doctor appointments. As the assistant principal kept talking, Asher's tardiness and absences began to take on a new light.

"Anyway, so given all of that," she concluded, "I think we need to go ahead and waive the disciplinary consequences in this case. Especially at a school like ours, I think showing that mercy is the appropriate thing to do."

I nodded slowly, considering what I had just learned. "I understand," I finally said, adjusting the legal pad on my clipboard. "I'll take it from here."

WITNESS AND DISCIPLINE

In my frustration with the seeming inconsistency between disciplinary policy and the conversation with administration, I overlooked the delicate disciplinary balancing act that often takes place. I, like others, allowed my own experiences as a Catholic school student and what I assumed a Catholic school to be to frame my expectations. The clear behavioral expectations and specific consequences in place created, for me, a false sense that discipline is black and white. Even within a faith that recognizes objective Truth, such an understanding of Truth nevertheless exists within a world that presents shades of gray. What I failed to acknowledge was the potential for compassion and witness when dealing with these gray-area moments.

In an instance like Asher's, the exception to a disciplinary policy wasn't based on a whim or on favoritism, per se; rather, it was grounded in an understanding of and appreciation for what are often referred to as the corporal works of mercy: feeding the hungry, giving drink to the thirsty, sheltering the homeless, visiting the sick, visiting the imprisoned, and burying the dead. In addition to supporting Asher's upholding of the commandment to "honor thy father and mother," the school acknowledged his role in ministering to the sick—in this case, his father.

Reminding all stakeholders that the locus for this approach to discipline lies in a Catholic anthropology would be beneficial to students, parents, and faculty. Faculty preplanning often includes reminders regarding disciplinary procedures and exhortations to ensure their consistent application. What would be helpful, though, and possibly result in additional "buy-in" from faculty, is a clearer explanation of how the student conduct expectations and the disciplinary infrastructure of the school connect to the school's mission. Start-of-year assemblies for students, meanwhile, are straightforward in their reiteration of perennial infractions: haircuts, shirttails, shoes, etc. Incorporating explanations for these policies and consequences might help to "soften the blow" by giving students context for the rules that govern their day-to-day school experience. To do so also would be a step toward the specific virtue pedagogy suggested by Lapsley and Kelley.

This is faith in action. This is witness. This is what we should be doing and articulating as clearly as we can as often as we can.

CHAPTER 8

CULTURE IN THE CLASSROOM

"I just don't understand why you're trying to proselytize my child," the parent said, tears welling up in her eyes. "I sent my children here specifically so they wouldn't have to put up with that kind of thing. This is supposed to be a secular school."

"We're a non-sectarian school, not a secular school," I said, trying to maintain the neutrality in my voice even as the frustration began to rise in the back of my throat.

"I don't know what that means," the parent shot back at me. She sniffed as she dabbed at her eyes with a tissue. Leah leaned forward, meeting my eyes and subtly shaking her head. I closed my half-open mouth and sat back in my own chair, letting her take over the conversation. The meeting had been tense from the start, but things were beginning to turn combative. Both of us wanted to resolve the issue and go home.

"Mrs. Smith," she began, "I understand you're frustrated. Our unit on origin stories included the book of Genesis, true, but we also incorporated selections from the Qur'an. Since one of the goals of this course is to answer the question 'What does it mean to be human?' we're exploring a wide variety of ways people have tried to answer that question over time. That includes looking to various traditions' sacred texts, but we're teaching them as literature and as historical artifacts."

"I just... I spent my whole childhood having that stuff crammed down my throat, and I promised myself I would never subject my own children to that," Mrs. Smith said.

Leah and I sat quietly while Mrs. Smith pulled another tissue from the box I'd placed on the table between us. I focused my gaze on my hands folded tightly in my lap, my fingernails digging into my palm. The tension in my collarbones refused to release. *One day, I will teach in a school where I won't have to justify the cultural references that I make in my classroom,* I promised myself.

THE CALL TO ENGAGE THE CULTURE

As much as I loved teaching that class in my first high school teaching job, I occasionally had to field questions like Mrs. Smith's. The class's whole focus was cultural engagement. Working from the premise of "text as cultural artifact," we examined the way specific cultural moments in the Western tradition engaged with and tried to answer the question "What does it mean to be human?"

We tried to answer the question largely without broaching the topic of faith in anything other than a vaguely anthropological way. In fact, the unit that caused Mrs. Smith so much heartache was intended primarily as background information so that students would have a better understanding of the Christian allusions in the art and literature of the medieval and Renaissance West. Something always felt a little hollow in this approach, though. Perhaps that's because one of the ways people and cultures try to answer the question "What does it mean to be human?" is through faith. The Catholic school, then, has a unique position to engage with culture at the very nexus of its most essential question.

Catholicism has strived to engage with culture since its beginnings, and the Catholic Church's rich intellectual history is well documented (so much so that I won't attempt to summarize it here for fear of not doing it justice). Whether engaging with the Ephesians or transcribing ancient manuscripts in medieval scriptoria, the intersections of culture, education, and faith are inherent in the Catholic tradition. Today, the most potent intersections of these entities occur in Catholic schools.

The Vatican's Sacred Congregation for Catholic Education has regularly asserted the importance of the Catholic school, particularly since the Second Vatican Council in the mid-twentieth century. In its 1977 document *The Catholic School*, the Sacred Congregation for Catholic Education declared that "in the course of the centuries 'while constantly holding to the fullness of divine truth' the Church has progressively used the sources and the means of culture in order to deepen her understanding of revelation and promote constructive dialogue with the world." Regarding objections made to Catholic schools, "many people, both inside and outside the Church, motivated by a mistaken sense of the lay role in secular society, attack Catholic schools as institutions. They do not admit that, apart from the individual witness of her members, the Church also may offer witness by means of her institutions, e.g., those dedicated to the search for truth or to works of charity." The document includes an entire section focused on the integration of faith and culture that concludes by highlighting the vital importance of the integration of faith and culture in the teachers themselves, calling them to "reveal the Christian message not only by word but also by every gesture of their behavior."

Catholic schools have always understood that part of their mission is to familiarize students with the wealth of human knowledge that makes up culture and understand that knowledge through a Catholic worldview. Furthermore, the Catholic Church itself recognizes and endorses this approach as integral to the mission and purpose of the Catholic school. In an increasingly globalized and secularized world, though, how should a Catholic school respond?

ENGAGING TWENTY-FIRST CENTURY CULTURE: SOME PERSPECTIVES

A myriad of perspectives exist regarding the challenges schools face today as they attempt to respond to the current cultural moment. Some, such as that of Daniel E. Burns, highlight the specific challenges raised by the ubiquity of technology, and more specifically, social media, in life and culture. Taking Yuval Levin's framework for understanding social and political institutions as "'molds' of character formation, not merely as 'platforms' for members' individual self-aggrandizement," Burns proposes that mission-driven K–12 schools lie at the nexus of character formation and cultural zeitgeist and therefore have the potential to stand fast against the trends of a moment.

Burns argues that an overwhelming amount of "noise" exists in today's cultural milieu, particularly when examining current institutions and platforms. One of his main critiques is the destructive, narcissistic bent to much of the social media currently being created and consumed. And he's right, to a point. But to actively eschew such an approach also runs the risk of turning away from an opportunity to "meet students where they are"—or, in this case, meet the culture where it is. If Jesus spent time among the marginalized in society, choosing the sick, the poor, and the ostracized over the "elites," as Burns calls them, then it stands to reason that Catholic entities can and should engage with people where they congregate (whether physically or virtually).

Others, such as Robert Mixa, echo the Catholic Church's own language regarding the impetus and value of Catholic education's approach to cultural engagement. In some ways, Mixa appears to agree with Burns; where Burns brings to the fore the shortcomings of a technology-obsessed twenty-first century and its potential to degrade the moral formation of future generations, Mixa highlights the influence of this hyperawareness of technological advancement within the K–12 classroom. Pointing out Catholic schools' potential financial limitations when it comes to employment of the most up-to-date, state-of-the-art technology, Mixa argues that Catholic schools should (re)commit themselves to "having the best humanistic education possible." Such a (re) commitment would be "less a drawing-in as a leading-out to encounter reality in its perennial expression, training students to take delight in the transcendentals shining forth in creation."

This is where Catholic schools have an opportunity, and many of them are already engaging with this chance: using the current modes of cultural discourse, including social media, to provide a witness to the culture. In this way, they can follow the lead of institutions like Word on Fire, whose landing page on its website declares its intention to "proclaim Christ in the culture" by "us[ing] contemporary forms of media and innovative communication technologies [...] to be most effective in this mission." While there may also be student enrollment and faculty recruiting advantages to a social media presence, ultimately those schools choosing to engage with social media are effectively positioned to accomplish what Burns, Mixa, and the Vatican itself desire: to engage with the particularities of twenty-first century culture while also attempting to promote "constructive dialogue with the world."

Amid these conversations, the Catholic Church continues to build upon its rich tradition as it meets the challenges of the modern world. In response to the globalization of the twenty-first century, the Catholic Church has responded with a call not just to engage the culture in Catholic schools, but to do so with an increasing recognition of the importance of what it calls "intercultural dialogue." In fact, the

2013 document "Educating to Intercultural Dialogue in Catholic Schools: Living in Harmony for a Civilization of Love" acknowledges the role of education in such a project; it is "precisely to promote dialogue [...] helping people to revisit their own cultures, with the cultures of others as their starting point." Furthermore, the Church recognizes that the search for meaning lies at the heart of the educational ethos. One of the ways to work toward understanding that meaning is from encounter and engagement with the unfamiliar, using "the awareness of one's own tradition and culture [as] the starting point."

Another way to think of this necessary encounter and engagement is through witness.

DIFFERENT SETTING, SAME QUESTION?

Vivian looked up as I walked into the department office. I had just finished teaching my last class of the day, and I was looking forward to a quiet planning period so I could try to make a dent in the growing stack of assignments needing to be graded. "Hi, neighbor!" she said as I slid past her and sat down next to her. She moved a stack of her own papers that had spilled over onto my desk.

"Howdy, neighbor," I said, smiling back. "How's it going?"

The expression on her face changed as she spun her desk chair around to face me. "Well, I want to let you know I just got out of a meeting. It turns out that a parent of one of your students has some concerns about *Brave New World* and has written a letter to the chaplain about it."

"Oh, really?" My eyebrows furrowed as I considered what Vivian had just said. "When did this happen? Why did they go straight to the chaplain first? Why am I just now hearing about this?"

"From what I understand, this has happened before. It could be that they felt more comfortable going to the chaplain first, since they've had these conversations in the past." Her tone was intended to be soothing, I knew, but it had little effect. I carefully avoided eye contact while trying to quell my rising anger. "I have a copy of the letter here," she continued. "I think it's okay for you to read it." She handed it to me.

It was two pages, front and back, of single-spaced text. The content of the letter was almost breathtaking in its scope: drawing from Catholic Church teaching, book review websites, and curricular resources, it questioned broad thematic issues and drew close attention to specific passages. Rhetorically, it appealed to logic, ethics, and emotion. It also acknowledged potential counterarguments contained in the rationale that already existed for teaching the novel. I had never seen anything like it.

I rocked back and forth in my desk chair as I skimmed the letter, conscious of my efforts to keep my breathing regular even as anxiety began to make my scalp tingle. Then, I turned back to the first page and read the whole thing a second time.

"So, what are we going to do?" I said to Vivian, trying not to sound plaintive. I fiddled with the pages of the letter, side-eyeing them as I tried to process what I'd read.

"I have a follow-up meeting with admin later this week, so I'll let you know what's decided," she said. "You won't have to worry about it."

Be careful what you wish for, I thought to myself. *Maybe having the opportunity to explain your decisions isn't so bad, after all.*

ENGAGING CULTURE IN THE CLASSROOM THROUGH WITNESS

The situation regarding *Brave New World* left me feeling betrayed in a way that I hadn't expected. After years of convincing myself that teaching in a Catholic school would alleviate the stress I felt when fielding parental questions about faith and literature, I was surprised by this recurrence of familiar sensations. At the time, I perceived such encounters as a challenge of my professional judgment and qualification. I bristled at the thought of others calling the work I had put into my education and preparation into doubt.

Most surprising, though, was the feeling that I had been denied an opportunity that I realized I'd taken for granted before. Although I was still apprehensive about face-to-face meetings with parents and administrators, I also was excited about how I intended to put Huxley's novel into conversation with what I knew my students had learned in their theology, science, and history classes. I was looking forward to building on the rapport I had fostered all semester with my students as I encouraged them to consider how they could use even the difficult passages in the novel to understand contemporary issues.

Though I had not yet learned the phrase "intercultural dialogue," I had already intuited the value of bringing culture, education, and faith into conversation in my classroom. The interdisciplinary approach I learned through working with Leah continued to ground my pedagogy. If anything, I felt even more confident in its employment in my work as a Catholic school teacher. As I considered my own curriculum and looked for continuities over time, I found myself returning to the same question:

What does it mean to be human in the twenty-first century cultural moment?

- To be inundated with information, often by way of novel and recent technological developments
- To struggle to discern what it means for something to be "truth" or "fact"—and to know who or what to trust as a result
- To encounter difference, dissonance, and disorder

Responding to these facets of the contemporary human experience in the classroom is both challenging and invigorating. During whole-class and small-group discussions this year, I have found myself asking students questions about how Church teaching and scripture could help them understand the issues they encounter in the works we read. When discussing *Pride and Prejudice*, for example, students often will want to say that Darcy has too much pride and Elizabeth Bennet has too much prejudice. However, the more I teach the novel, the more apparent it becomes that pride and prejudice are two sides of the same coin, and both central characters struggle with them. Even though the novel is more than two hundred years old, the pride and prejudice at the heart of the novel stem from a series of missteps rooted in the same issues my students face today: confronting information overload, discerning truth, and navigating dissonance.

Moreover, it is only once the characters both learn humility (Darcy through the rejection of his marriage proposal and the subsequent letter he writes to Elizabeth, and Elizabeth through making herself reconsider how she has misjudged Darcy after reading the letter) that they are able to build a relationship that is eventually successful. Humility as the corresponding virtue to the sin of pride—indeed, as its antidote—has become one of the lessons I try to incorporate into our discussions. While this instruction rarely takes the form of lecture, highlighting the development of my own understanding of the novel has helped my students to feel more comfortable with taking risks in their analysis and making interdisciplinary, relational connections to the text.

When done well through the fostering of relationships between students and faculty, the intercultural dialogue in the Catholic school classroom can extend beyond the immediately curricular. During Susannah's thirteen-year career as a Catholic school educator, she told me she has encountered many moments where her job description as "Teacher/Minister" comes into play in the classroom.

Students will sometimes come to her classes and approach her with questions about her responses to hot-button issues. As even "classic" works of literature broach the same topics, the questions are germane to the text at hand, though with ramifications beyond the text itself. When she fields these questions, she often responds with a frank but not unkind, "What does it matter what I think?" On occasions when her students press the question, she says, "Okay, but I'm just one person. I'm hoping you know what the Catechism [of the Catholic Church] says about that." They usually respond in the affirmative, at which point Susannah says, "Well, we all have free will [...] but it also sounds like you know the rule. And the rule applies to everybody." Rather than rancor, she told me, these conversations are met with resolution and clarity that underscores the strength of her relationship with her students.

To be in education at this moment is to be keenly aware of these manifestations of essential questions—indeed, of *the* essential question. To know how to respond to this question of being human in the twenty-first century cultural moment and how to live with the potential answers to this question requires community and witness. Once again, the Catholic Church recognizes the relational imperative when it proclaims that relationships among individuals ultimately expand outward to awareness of relationships among academic disciplines. The best approach, furthermore, relies on dialogue—"the only possible solution," according to the Church herself.

WITNESS AND THE CLASSROOM

At the College Board's Advanced Placement Exam Reading one summer, I happened to fall into step with another teacher as we made our way to one of the nightly program workshops. Noticing the name of a Catholic school on her name badge, I struck up a conversation with her as we searched for the correct meeting room. That conversation, which continued for another two hours after we left the program workshop, was a beautiful testament to the power of Catholic education. As she put it, "Being Catholic is a way of life. It's been great. It's been very, very fulfilling." At face value, she was referring to her own journey to Catholicism as an adult. In a broader sense, though, she also pointed to something I had been trying to articulate since beginning this project: to be a Catholic educator is to have the profound honor to show students how to live a Catholic life—integrated, fully realized, embracing the intersections of culture, education, and faith.

In order to guide students toward embracing the intersections of culture, education, and faith, schools must be willing to engage with and respond to the voices making themselves heard in the current cultural moment as part of helping students understand the reality they face. This is not necessarily done with an eye always toward endorsement of the cultural moment per se, but with an eye toward comprehending so as to encounter and respond to it confidently and competently. Teachers, in line with the Catholic Church's statements on the role of Catholic educators in the process, can and should lead by example—by exploring these questions and engaging in this intercultural dialogue "in real time" with their students, thereby providing their own witness to the process of encounter.

In a real sense, witness in the classroom is the culmination of everything this book has tried to articulate. I have realized that my ability to live and teach at the intersections of culture, education, and faith has grown out of my own personal and professional formation: through the reading I have done, the Bible studies I have joined, and the conversations I've had with colleagues during faculty meetings and retreats. The more comfortable I have become integrating my faith life and learning into the classroom, the more authentic the connections I encourage my students to see have been. The development has occurred subtly and gradually; nevertheless, it has been transformative.

I sincerely hope all Catholic educators remain open to such transformation.

CONCLUSION

I started writing this book for all the wrong reasons.

I was angry and frustrated by the vagaries of the teacher certification process, even though I had known when I accepted my current position that I would have to pursue certification in order to remain an employee. I was disillusioned by the seeming disconnect between the image I had built up of what I thought Catholic education was and the reality of being a teacher in a Catholic school. I was exasperated by the administrative minutiae that comes with the classroom territory, particularly because it encroached on what I really wanted to do: read books and discuss them and hopefully get my students to see why understanding storytelling is essential to understanding humanity. I was disappointed by our current cultural moment, particularly how it seems to put so little value on the things that bring me joy and make me feel like I have a purpose. I had fantasized about transitioning to a different career path that could still be education-adjacent, and I hoped writing a book could get me there.

I was full of vim and vigor and righteous indignation. I was also incredibly selfish.

Amid this emotional maelstrom, I began to write. Meanwhile, it was the witness of my colleagues and students that sustained me. My principal made room for me in her busy schedule to listen to my concerns, always making sure to ask how things were going in my personal and spiritual life. My colleagues made countless offers of assistance: making copies, ensuring substitute teachers could find the materials that my students needed when I couldn't be in class, and keeping me in their prayers. A few of them met me outside of work hours to listen when I needed an ear and make sure that I ate. My students, though they might not ever realize it, grounded me when I otherwise might have been totally adrift. Knowing I had the chance to share my love of literature with them, getting to encourage them through their final year of high school, and learning from them as we navigated lesson plans and COVID-19 quarantines and last-minute schedule changes became my anchor during a sometimes tumultuous writing process.

Perhaps most of all, though, recognizing God's work through them—seeing for myself the power of evangelizing by example—brought to light the power of witness in Catholic schools. It became clear to me that what we were doing was exactly what the Catholic Church's Sacred Congregation for Catholic Education encourages its Catholic schools to do: "to provide a place for the critical communication of human culture and the total formation of the individual, it works toward this goal guided by its Christian vision of reality 'through which our cultural heritage acquires its special place in the total vocational life of man.'"

The problem wasn't only, or even mostly, with the system. The problem was also with my own myopia.

***

After wading into this project, some of the decisions I had initially railed against seem more understandable. There are always exchanges that must be made. There are always compromises to be reached. Catholic schools, in many ways and in many different forums, are actively navigating these exchanges and compromises. Some of these exchanges and compromises also require that Catholic schools reaffirm their mission, and those compromises must be acknowledged and addressed.

When enrollment drops beyond whatever operational margin has been set, as has happened in some Catholic dioceses and independent Catholic schools, these schools must determine how best to attract and retain families within the school community. For other schools, the pressure to appeal to a broader audience results in having to ask serious questions regarding the viability of downplaying Catholic identity for enrollment management purposes. At other times, Catholic schools must reconcile their commitment to providing Catholic education to any family who wishes it for their children regardless of their ability to pay with the financial realities of maintaining staff and facilities.

When a desire to be responsible stewards of financial resources, particularly regarding staff and facilities, leads to the examination of funding possibilities outside of tuition, some Catholic schools find themselves eligible for state or federal funding allocated for private school use. Taking advantage of these resources, however, may come with stipulations about the use of these funds. Restrictions often prevent schools from using the funds to aid the Catholic mission of the school, particularly regarding the religious education at its core. In these instances, funding opportunities may result in their use for secular aims—which, while they may provide practical tools for the classroom setting, might not meet a school's most pressing professional development needs.

When diocesan and independent Catholic schools find themselves confronted with the perception that independent school faculty aren't as "qualified" as their public school counterparts, schools may need to reexamine their certification requirements. One option for counteracting this perception lies in requiring teacher certification for instructional staff. If a teacher certification program with a religious instruction component does not exist, then schools may opt to accept certification through a secular program. Furthermore, once teachers possess the same credentials as their public school counterparts, the desire for responsible financial stewardship sometimes results in an inability to provide competitive salaries. The result, unfortunately, is the loss of good, qualified faculty.

When the current cultural moment requires direct engagement in the classroom, Catholic schools may find themselves navigating issues, ideas, or positions that are critical of or counter to a Catholic anthropology. The Catholic Church itself emphasizes the vital role its schools have as centers for dialogue and the intersections of culture and faith. The rich tradition of the Catholic Church also makes available plentiful resources for approaching contentious topics within the cultural moment. Even so, facing the headwinds of the moment also necessitates candid considerations of how best to clarify the Catholic position without falling prey to perceptions of rigidity that stifle rather than encourage dialogue and understanding. In addition, ensuring all faculty members—regardless of religious or political affiliation—are committed to engaging the cultural moment from a Catholic anthropology can become its own balancing act.

***

I remain convinced that educators in Catholic schools need better catechesis—instruction in the core beliefs within Catholicism—in order to fully appreciate and carry out the mission of their employer. Understanding how to incorporate such catechesis into our faculty professional development in a meaningful way is key to the continued success of Catholic schools. Ensuring that mission influences all aspects of the work faculty undertake with their students in a way that feels organic and comfortable is the next step. This integration is what distinguishes Catholic schools from other schools; a rich and scholastic faith-filled tradition grounds Catholic institutions.

Moreover, this integration lies at the heart of what I mean by *witness*. It has the potential to be both more intentional and less overt than some professional development initiatives that might currently be in place in some Catholic schools. This is why I am trying to make a distinction between what I mean and "evangelization," which can have its own extraverted, structured, and conversion-focused implications. (Not that any of those things is bad—quite the contrary—but for faculty and schools that might not have held extended, explicit discussions about the Catholic identity of the school in the past, a term that suggests listening could prove more palatable.) It requires that faculty first feel comfortable talking with their colleagues about their lived experiences, and then that they feel comfortable talking about "The Big Questions": God, the meaning of life, what it means to be Catholic—whether Roman Catholic or "catholic" simply in the sense of "universal."

Catholic schools can encourage dialogue through interpersonal communication in any number of ways with varying degrees of formality. Voluntary faculty small groups who get together outside of school hours for fellowship is one way to begin the process of witness. Developing a faculty-wide, faith-based mentorship program and then creating opportunities (aside from PD days, teacher workdays, etc.) for colleagues to meet would allow the type of personal witness that can strengthen collegiality and Catholicity. Developing space during faculty meetings for faith discussions, while more formal than either of the previous two suggestions, nevertheless can provide a starting point for important discussions that must take place before the faculty can witness to their students.

I admire and applaud schools that already engage in efforts to foster witness among their faculty, staff, students, and families. These are important endeavors, and those who have taken up the call to revitalize Catholic education should feel heartened by the example they have set for other schools to follow. My own school has undertaken some of these initiatives, giving me inspiration to share their efforts with others. At the same time, I will confess that almost all my experience within Catholic schools—whether as student or as teacher—has been within a single diocese, in one part of the country. Therefore, my own witness is somewhat limited. The dynamism of the Catholic community across the country undoubtedly is reflected in its own efforts, and I sincerely hope I can continue to learn from other teachers and administrators who have found ways to witness to their students.

***

Ultimately, I have learned that Catholic schools are more dynamic and more complicated than I had previously wanted to acknowledge. The schools themselves must navigate the winds of the current cultural moment while remaining true to Church teaching and keeping the doors open. The day-to-day operations must be in the world while being careful not to be wholly of the world. And while we can continue to work toward ensuring students have a more solid understanding of the tenets of Catholicism, we can do a more deliberate job of giving teachers the tools they need to be more intentional in conveying to their students how Catholic faith intersects with everything from literature to logarithms, from Beethoven to business ethics. I also think that living our faith—living our vocation—is most important of all. It's a both/and, not an either/or, proposition I'm suggesting. I'm certain I don't have all the answers, but I want to add my voice to the chorus calling for an earnest (re)engagement with the conversation.

A diocesan administrator once referred to the "educational apostolate" during an all-diocese in-service. The phrase has stayed with me. If the original apostles followed Jesus, learned from him, and then shared their witness—their lived experiences and the truth of the teachings they received—with others, then the phrase seems particularly apt for today's Catholic school educators. The work of revitalizing Catholic schools begins with a renewed commitment on the part of its faculty: to themselves, to each other, to their students, and to God.

We must not only save minds. We must also save souls.

ACKNOWLEDGMENTS

"Become a published author" has been at the top of my "'One Day' List" (a term I prefer to "bucket list") for as long as I can remember. Now this lifelong goal of mine has become a reality, and I could not have done it without the love, guidance, and support of more people than I have space here to name. With apologies for any inadvertent omissions, I would like to give special recognition to the following:

To my immediate family, especially my parents, sisters, and husband—you are the reason this little book has made its way into the world. Thank you, always and forever, for believing in me and doing everything in your power to make my dreams come true. I love you more than you will ever know.

Thank you to the colleagues, professional connections, experts, and mentors who have shared their stories with me. Your candor and perspectives have helped me to refine my own thoughts about revitalizing Catholic education, and I am grateful for your willingness to entrust your words and witness to my pen. I hope I have done justice to you.

I owe a debt of gratitude to the Book Creators team and New Degree Press for helping me navigate the book-writing and publishing processes: Eric Koester; Haley Newlin; Kyra Dawkins; my developmental editor, Alexander Pyles; and my marketing and revisions editor, Cynthia Tucker. Thanks to your instruction and encouragement, I know now that I am never writing alone.

Finally, thank you to everyone who has believed in *Saving Minds, Saving Souls* throughout this journey. Those of you who supported its publication by promoting and contributing to the presale campaign have helped to make this project a reality: Susan and David Carpenter, Dante Guanlao, Lou Tate, Cara de Dios, Victoria Nixon Bailess, Catherine and Tate Blenke, Ashley Whitmire, Theresa Morrow, John Paul Price, Casey Carpenter Jarman, Dr. Victoria R. Farmer, Jon Westcott, Erik H. Carpenter, Kim Yates, Sara Ciskie, Ben Dawkins, Katie Malec, Lindsey Hayes, Elizabeth Buyarski, Lynne and Tony Cerniglia, Eric Koester, Kristen Nicole Cerniglia, Debra C. Callaway, Kimberly Meade, Mary Ashby, Frank Morelli, Kevin Pilcher, Lauren Bartleson, Kristin Satterfield, Mary Nappi, Robin Terry, Allison Albert, Lauren Kim, Meredith McCall, Peggy and Gordon Morrow, Kristin H. Nelson, Beverly Jodi Gucer, Savannah Cerniglia, Sue and Joe T. Cerniglia, Jamie Reger, Lauren Ward, Michael R. Burns, Shelby Cerniglia, Darlene Whitmire, Erin McKenna, Debra Jean Dowlen, Jim Turner, Anne Chadwick Perry, Joseph O'Farrell, Anne Pilcher, Andrew Gunsch, and Maj. Bankers.

APPENDIX

INTRODUCTION

Barron, Bishop Robert. "287: The Future of Catholic Schools." Produced by Word on Fire. Word on Fire Show. June 7, 2021. Podcast, MP3 format, 31:42. https://www.wordonfire.org/videos/wordonfire-show/episode287/.

Lovett, Ian. "Catholic Schools Are Losing Students at Record Rates, and Hundreds Are Closing." *Wall Street Journal* online. May 10, 2021. https://www.wsj.com/articles/catholic-schools-are-losing-students-at-record-rates-and-hundreds-are-closing-11620651600.

Miksic, Mai. "Is the 'Catholic School Effect' Real? New Research Challenges the Catholic Primary School Advantage." *The Institute*. Johns Hopkins University School of Education Institute for Education Policy. June 19, 2014. https://edpolicy.education.jhu.edu/is-the-catholic-school-effect-real-new-research-challenges-the-catholic-primary-school-advantage/.

Porter-Magee, Kathleen. "Catholic on the Inside: Putting Values Back at the Center of Education Reform." Manhattan Institute for Policy Research. December 12, 2019. https://www.

manhattan-institute.org/traditional-charter-schools-lessons-from-catholic-schools#notes.

Ray, Brian D. "Homeschooling: The Research." Research Facts on Homeschooling. National Home Education Research Institute. March 26, 2022. https://www.nheri.org/research-facts-on-homeschooling/.

White, Jamison, and Matt Hieronimus. "1. How Many Charter Schools and Students Are There?" National Alliance for Public Charter Schools. February 9, 2022. https://data.publiccharters.org/digest/charter-school-data-digest/how-many-charter-schools-and-students-are-there/.

CHAPTER 1

Every Student Succeeds Act, Public Law 114-95, 129 Stat. 1802 (2015). https://www.congress.gov/114/plaws/publ95/PLAW-114publ95.pdf.

"History and Evolution of Public Education in the US." Center on Education Policy. The George Washington University Graduate School for Education & Human Development, 2020. https://files.eric.ed.gov/fulltext/ED606970.pdf.

National Association of Secondary School Principals. "Every Student Succeeds Act (ESSA): Title II—Preparing, Training, and Recruiting High Quality Teachers, Principals, or Other School Leaders." National Association of Secondary School Teachers, 2022. https://www.nassp.org/a/title-ii-preparing-training-and-recruiting-high-quality-teachers-principals-or-other-school-leaders/.

"Religious Landscape Study." Pew Research Center. Accessed May 18, 2022. https://www.pewresearch.org/religion/religious-landscape-study/.

"The Elementary and Secondary Education Act (ESEA), as Amended by the Every Student Succeeds Act (ESSA): A

Primer." Congressional Research Service. Updated April 20, 2022. https://crsreports.congress.gov/product/pdf/R/R45977.

McDonald, Dale, and Margaret Schultz. *U.S. Catholic Elementary and Secondary Schools 2020–2021: The Annual Statistical Report on Schools, Enrollment and Staffing*. National Catholic Educators Association, 2021.

"Update: ESEA Reauthorization | Every Student Succeeds Act." The Hunt Institute. Duke University Sanford School of Public Policy. Accessed June 22, 2022. http://www.hunt-institute.org/wp-content/uploads/2016/01/Update_ESEAReauthorization_Final_ForWeb.pdf.

Wodon, Quentin. "Heterogeneity in Parental Priorities for What Children Should Learn in Schools and Potential Implications for the Future of Catholic Schools." *Journal of Catholic Education* 25, no. 1 (2022): 178–205. Accessed June 22, 2022. http://dx.doi.org/10.15365/joce.2501082022.

CHAPTER 2

Bamford, Greg. "Getting to the Point in School Mission Statements." *Independent School*, Spring 2020. National Association of Independent Schools. Accessed May 25, 2022. https://www.nais.org/magazine/independent-school/spring-2020/getting-to-the-point-in-school-mission-statements/.

Congregation for Catholic Education. *The Catholic School on the Threshold of the Third Millennium*. Dec. 28, 1997. Accessed May 25, 2022. https://www.vatican.va/roman_curia/congregations/ccatheduc/documents/rc_con_ccatheduc_doc_27041998_school2000_en.html.

"Fallacy." Merriam-Webster. Merriam-Webster, Inc., 2022. https://www.merriam-webster.com/dictionary/fallacy.

Gow, Peter. "Independent School Mission Statements and Missions." Education Week. Editorial Projects in Education, Inc. July 18,

2014. https://www.edweek.org/education/opinion-independent-school-mission-statements-and-missions/2014/07.
Hart, Mark. "Saints in the Making." *Ascension Blog.* Ascension: The Faith Formation Leader. Ascension Press. Nov. 1, 2017. https://media.ascensionpress.com/2017/11/01/saints-making/.
"James 5:13." BibleHub: Search, Read, Study the Bible in Many Languages. Accessed June 25, 2022. https://biblehub.com/james/5-13.htm.
Kotkins, Skip. "Are Mission Statements Passé?" The Puzzle: Blog. Carney Sandoe & Associates. Dec. 3, 2018. https://www.carneysandoe.com/blog-post/are-mission-statements-passe.
The Sacred Congregation for Catholic Education. *The Catholic School.* March 19, 1977. Accessed May 25, 2022. https://www.vatican.va/roman_curia/congregations/ccatheduc/documents/rc_con_ccatheduc_doc_19770319_catholic-school_en.html.

CHAPTER 3

Epps, Tyler. "Humanities and Social Sciences Careers." Best Colleges. May 6, 2022. https://www.bestcolleges.com/careers/humanities-and-social-sciences/.
Indeed Editorial Team. "13 Jobs for Humanities Majors." February 10, 2022. https://www.indeed.com/career-advice/finding-a-job/humanities-major-jobs.
"Humanities Indicators: Bachelor's Degrees in the Humanities." American Academy of Arts and Sciences, 2002. https://www.amacad.org/humanities-indicators/higher-education/bachelors-degrees-humanities.
National Association of Independent Schools. "Career Center." Accessed May 17, 2022. https://careers.nais.org/jobs.
National Center for Education Statistics. "Table 322.10. Bachelor's Degrees Conferred by Postsecondary Institutions, by Field of Study: Selected Years, 1970–1 through 2019–20." US Depart-

ment of Education. Accessed May 25, 2022. https://nces.ed.gov/programs/digest/d19/tables/dt19_322.10.asp.

"Romans 8:30." Bible Hub: Search, Read, Study the Bible in Many Languages. Accessed May 25, 2022. https://biblehub.com/romans/8-30.htm.

University of Phoenix. "Why a Career Change into Teaching may be the Best Fit for You." Mashable. Mashable, Inc. May 26, 2017. https://mashable.com/ad/article/education-career-change.

CHAPTER 4

"2022 Teacher Certification (Complete Guide)." TEACH.org. Accessed May 25, 2022. https://www.teach.org/becoming-teacher/teaching-certification.

Flaherty, Colleen. "Death by a Thousand Cuts." Inside Higher Ed. October 28, 2020. https://www.insidehighered.com/news/2020/10/28/teacher-education-programs-continue-suffer-death-thousand-cuts.

King, Jacqueline E., and Jessica Yin. "The Alternative Teacher Certification Sector Outside of Higher Education: 2022 Update." Center for American Progress. June 7, 2022. https://www.americanprogress.org/article/the-alternative-teacher-certification-sector-outside-higher-education/.

Mikulecky, Marga, Gina Shkodriani, and Abby Wilner. "Alternative Certification: A Growing Trend to Address the Teacher Shortage." Education Commission of the States. December 2004. https://files.eric.ed.gov/fulltext/ED484845.pdf.

"National Board Certification." National Board for Professional Teaching Standards. NBPTS, 2022. https://www.nbpts.org.

"Teacher Education: From Revolution to Evolution." Teacher Education Reinvented: Supporting Excellence in Teacher Education. NYU Steinhardt School of Culture, Education, and Human

Development. February 5, 2018. https://teachereducation.steinhardt.nyu.edu/teacher-training-evolution/.

CHAPTER 5

"Chapter 4—Catholic Identity and Religious Ed." Archdiocese of Los Angeles Administrative Handbook. The Roman Catholic Archbishop of Los Angeles, 2022. https://handbook.la-archdiocese.org/chapter-4/section-4-3/topic-4-3-10.

"Employee Faith Formation." St. Ignatius High School, Cleveland, Ohio. Accessed May 25, 2022. https://www.ignatius.edu/faith-in-action/spirituality-program-for-adults/employee-faith-formation?ext=.

"Faculty Faith Formation." Marist High School, Chicago, Illinois. Accessed May 25, 2022. https://www.marist.net/faith/faculty-faith-formation/.

Fussell, Ronald. "Feed My Sheep: A Framework for Lay Educator Faith Formation in Catholic Schools." *Journal of Catholic Education* 24, no. 1 (2021): 143–164. Accessed June 27, 2022. http://dx.doi.org/10.15365/joce.2401082021.

---. "Is Your Professional Formation Inspired?: Connecting Professional Learning with the Light of Faith." *Momentum*, Summer 2021. https://read.nxtbook.com/ncea/momentum/summer_2021/is_your_professional_formatio.html.

McDonald, Dale, and Margaret Schultz. *US Catholic Elementary and Secondary Schools 2020–2021: The Annual Statistical Report on Schools, Enrollment and Staffing.* National Catholic Educators Association, 2021.

"Sometimes a Step Forward Begins with a Retreat: A Guide to Planning the Staff Day of Reflection/Retreat." Toronto Catholic District School Board, 2007. Reprinted 2011. Accessed June 28, 2022. https://www.tcdsb.org/Board/NurturingOurCatholicCommunity/Documents/Retreat%20Planning.pdf.

The Sacred Congregation for Catholic Education. *Lay Catholics in Schools: Witnesses to the Faith*. October 15, 1982. Accessed May 25, 2022. https://www.vatican.va/roman_curia/congregations/ccatheduc/documents/rc_con_ccatheduc_doc_19821015_lay-catholics_en.html.

CHAPTER 6

Barron, Bishop Robert. "287: The Future of Catholic Schools." Produced by Word on Fire. Word on Fire Show. June 7, 2021. Podcast, MP3 format, 31:42. https://www.wordonfire.org/videos/wordonfire-show/episode287/.

---. "Evangelizing is Priority One: Bishop Barron Speaks to Catholic Educators." Word on Fire. February 23, 2021. Video, 43:57. https://www.wordonfire.org/videos/dialogues/evangelizing-is-priority-one-bishop-barron-speaks-to-catholic-educators/.

Congregation for Catholic Education. *Educating Today and Tomorrow: A Renewing Passion*. April 7, 2014. Accessed June 28, 2022. https://www.vatican.va/roman_curia/congregations/ccatheduc/documents/rc_con_ccatheduc_doc_20140407_educare-oggi-e-domani_en.html.

Fussell, Ronald. "Feed My Sheep: A Framework for Lay Educator Faith Formation in Catholic Schools." *Journal of Catholic Education* 24, no. 1 (2021): 143–164. Accessed June 27, 2022. http://dx.doi.org/10.15365/joce.2401082021.

Pietrantonio, Kyle, and Tim Uhl. "Episode 212: Kyle Pietrantonio and DIA Schools." *Catholic School Matters*. December 28, 2020. 37:49. https://catholicschoolmatters.libsyn.com/ep-212-catholic-school-matters.

Sanchez, Brandon. "Catholic Schools Challenged by Changing Demographics." *America: The Jesuit Review* online. America Press, Inc., September 21, 2018. https://www.americamagazine.org/faith/2018/09/21/catholic-schools-challenged-changing-demographics.

CHAPTER 7

Burnford, Thomas. "Here's How Catholic Schools Instill Self-Discipline." Thomas B. Fordham Institute. June 12, 2018. https://fordhaminstitute.org/national/commentary/heres-how-catholic-schools-instill-self-discipline.

Ferrisi, Sabrina. "Self-Discipline: The Catholic School Advantage." *National Catholic Register* online. June 28, 2018. https://www.ncregister.com/features/self-discipline-the-catholic-school-advantage.

Konzen, Joel, and Nick Carrier. "209: What It Means to 'Believe' in God." *The Best You Podcast with Nick Carrier.* September 28, 2020. 47:51. https://www.iheart.com/podcast/256-nick-carriers-best-you-pod-31113937/episode/209-bishop-joel-konzen-what-72007782/.

Lapsley, Daniel, and Katheryn Kelley. "On the Catholic Identity of Students and Schools: Value Propositions for Catholic Education." *Journal of Catholic Education* 25, no. 1 (2022): 159–177. http://dx.doi.org/10.15365/joce.2501072022.

Pondiscio, Robert. *How the Other Half Learns: Equality, Excellence, and the Battle Over School Choice.* New York: Avery Books, 2019.

Porter-Magee, Kathleen. "Catholic on the Inside: Putting Values Back at the Center of Education Reform." Manhattan Institute for Policy Research. December 12, 2019. https://www.manhattan-institute.org/traditional-charter-schools-lessons-from-catholic-schools#notes.

CHAPTER 8

Burns, Daniel E. "A Time to Build Schools." *Public Discourse.* The Witherspoon Institute. February 20, 2021. https://www.thepublicdiscourse.com/2021/02/74225/.

Congregation for Catholic Education. *Educating to Intercultural Dialogue in Catholic Schools: Living in Harmony for a Civilization of Love.* October 28, 2013. Accessed June 15, 2022. https://www.vatican.va/roman_curia/congregations/ccatheduc/documents/rc_con_ccatheduc_doc_20131028_dialogo-interculturale_en.html#_ftn20.

Mixa, Robert. "The Catholic School: Frontlines of Humanistic Education." *Word on Fire Institute.* Word on Fire. August 16, 2021. https://www.wordonfire.org/articles/fellows/the-catholic-school-frontlines-of-humanistic-education/.

The Sacred Congregation for Catholic Education. *The Catholic School.* March 19, 1977. Accessed May 25, 2022. https://www.vatican.va/roman_curia/congregations/ccatheduc/documents/rc_con_ccatheduc_doc_19770319_catholic-school_en.html.

CONCLUSION

The Sacred Congregation for Catholic Education. *The Catholic School.* March 19, 1977. Accessed May 25, 2022. https://www.vatican.va/roman_curia/congregations/ccatheduc/documents/rc_con_ccatheduc_doc_19770319_catholic-school_en.html.